Inner Guidance Made Simple through the Vibration of Color

Arlene Arnold

ColorCards,
Inner Guidance Made Simple
through the Vibration of Color
ISBN: 0-9649990-1-3

Printed in the USA
by
Transformational Tools Made Simple™
www.ArleneArnold.com
Arlene@ArleneArnold.com

Graphic Design, Illustration & Production
by Pam Horbett

Contents

Page

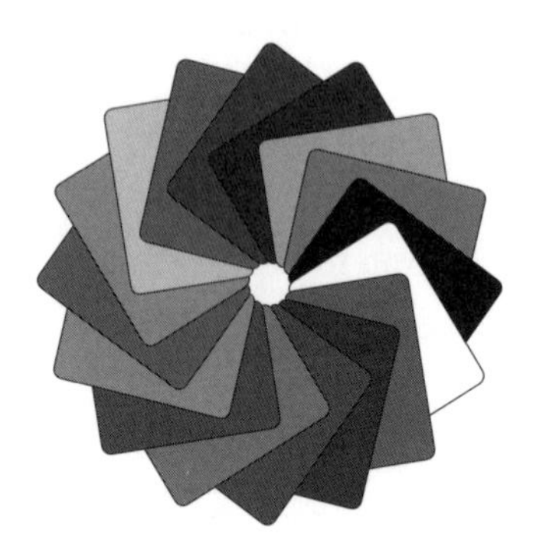

Acknowledgments

No project is ever the work of just one person. No book is every written solely by the author. I wish to acknowledge all the help I have received along the way. Since the first version of ColorCards™, I have taught many classes concerning the vibration of color. The questions and ideas that surfaced during these classes have been a great help. Members of a weekly spiritual growth group have given support, suggestions, and encouragement. I especially want to acknowledge the help of Diana Rayment from the group. Our joint venture into the realms of color taught us so much. Others include Peggy Smith, Nancy Brown, Doug Oliver, Tracey Morrisson, Barb Anderson, and Vernon Graves. In addition, I express deep appreciation for the assistance I have received from the Committee who work closely with my Inner Guidance.

At a point when I thought I might discontinue the ColorCards™, Joan Dever and others at Encouragement Lodge pointed out the value of what I had developed. That began my renewed resolve to take ColorCards™ to the next stage of its development. Thanks go to Donna Reis, who has introduced many to the ColorCards™ through her workshops and classes. I am grateful to David Young, Jane Lister Reis, Peggy Smith, Nancy Brown, and Diana Rayment for their help in editing the ColorCards™. Special thanks go to my graphic artist, Pam Horbett. With her help, the ColorCards™ have reached a new level of expression.

Introduction

Color has long been a medium of expression, from design in clothes, furniture, decorations, and landscaping to paintings, murals, and more. Much has been written about the effect of color on children, prison inmates, businesses, and the general public.

ColorCards™ allows you to experience this understanding of color in your own life. You have a built-in inner guidance system that responds to the vibration of color. Each color is designed to present to you an opportunity to learn about yourself. As you accept this learning, you develop inner strength and maturity. If you avoid or refuse these opportunities to learn, you are taken into circumstances and scenarios in your life that push you to reconsider.

The colors you like and enjoy around you tend to be those colors that present lessons you have mastered. Those colors you dislike, ignore, or avoid tend to be colors that present lessons you are still processing. Let's say that you love purple, but wouldn't think of surrounding yourself with yellow. You take a new job only to find that the room you will be working in is painted a bright yellow. Since you are new to the company and the people there, you don't dare suggest that they repaint the walls. I call this a "setup." You have offered yourself an opportunity to go through the lessons found in yellow. Through purple you have learned to trust and appreciate your intuition. You place great importance on your spiritual life. If it weren't that you have to provide the necessities of life, you wouldn't work at all. In this situation, yellow is teaching you that it is time to come down to Earth. Yellow is about learning to be practical and clear-minded while living as an empowered human being in the human situation. These two colors complete each other because they bring the balance needed to live your life fully.

Through the ColorCards™, you will discover the meaning of events in your life. You will be encouraged to pay attention to what is tapping you on the shoulder or demanding your attention in a stronger way. You will begin to appreciate how much you have grown and developed thus far in your life, and you will see more clearly what your life is all about.

ColorCards™ can be a fun, simple way to learn about you. This book and cards are also meant to be taken seriously. By using ColorCards™ as a spiritual tool, you open up to the possibility of tremendous transformation.

I encourage you to use the information wisely. As always, take what you learn into your heart center. Decide if what is presented fits for you on all levels. Be honest with yourself. Then, take what feels right and leave the rest. You and only you are responsible for your physical, emotional, mental, and spiritual wholeness.

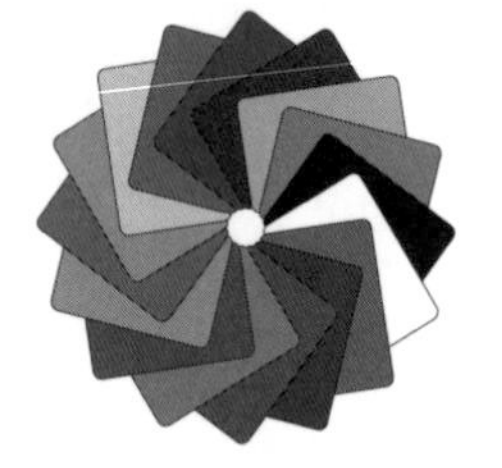

How to Use the ColorCards™

This book offers you information about each of the colors presented by the ColorCards™. This information is formatted in four categories:

Strengths, Lessons, Transformational Exercises, and Life Purpose

Strengths: You are unique. You come into this world with certain abilities and propensities in place. During your life, you develop what is innately part of you As you face difficulties in your life, you develop other aspects of yourself. These make up your "strengths."

Lessons: You are in a life process. Everyday you have the opportunity to become more authentically who you are. Sometimes you may miss the opportunity and sometimes you may avoid the opportunity out of fear or lack of understanding. Ultimately, the opportunity to learn about yourself comes back again and again in different forms. You can move to a new location, develop new friendships, or change to a new job; however, what you are learning will follow you until you are finished with it. ColorCards offers you the chance to consciously choose to move what you are learning into new or more expanded strengths within yourself.

Transformational Exercises: Moving forward in life requires you to understand your life better, and sometimes, it requires you to do something that brings about change in your life. The exercises for each color may move you more quickly from lesson to strength. The exercises may also help you more clearly understand the lesson you are working on.

Life Purpose: There is a reason why you came into this life. Discovering and living what sparks passion within you brings great satisfaction and sense of meaning to life. Each time you use the Life Purpose arrangement of cards, like discovering the many facets of a diamond, you see another aspect of your life path. As soon as you claim one, the next one reveals itself. Each of these facets makes up a clear, glimmering whole, allowing you to see your life direction more clearly.

Read the Book from Cover to Cover

Much may be gained by reading the book from cover to cover or by picking out specific colors you want to study. However, the following suggestions will allow you a variety of other ways to work with the book and cards.

Pick a Card

While looking at the colors of the cards, pick out your favorite. This may change from time to time, depending on what you are working on in your life. Turn to that color in the book and read what is said under "Strengths." The strengths of this color are what you have developed through time and what you have learned through your life experiences. Now, pick the color you like the least. Turn to that color in the book and read what is said about "Lessons." This color will indicate what you are still working with and what characteristics are still developing within you. Picking these two colors is a quick and easy way to see where you are on your journey.

Meditate on an Aspect Found in One Card

Pick a card without looking at the color. Read about this card or skim through the different aspects of this color. Pick out one thing that catches your attention. Place the card in front of you, color side up. Meditate on the color. Think about this aspect of the color that you picked out. Ask yourself what message is here for you in this color. Write about this aspect in your journal.

Pick a Card for the Day

Shuffle the cards. Focus on your desire to understand something important about your day. Without looking at the colors, intuitively pick a card. Turn to the book. Read the whole chapter about that color. Read with openness while allowing yourself to recognize the message for you in that chapter. You may find that you are to see your strength as it is revealed during that day, that you are challenged to learn something new that day, that you need the centering exercise that is suggested for that color, or that you are working on an aspect of your life purpose that day. This will help you to focus your attention on the meaning that is offered throughout the day.

Notice Colors Around You

Notice what colors you or someone else has chosen to wear. What do those colors mean? Notice colors in your home, in businesses, in schools, or most any place you are. Read about the colors in the ColorCard book. Why have these colors been chosen? How do these colors affect you and others? Make informed decisions about your use of color. Consult the ColorCards™ book before choosing your wardrobe, your car, your furniture, gifts you are giving, or anything that has to do with color. Be conscious of your use of color.

Finding Your Life Purpose

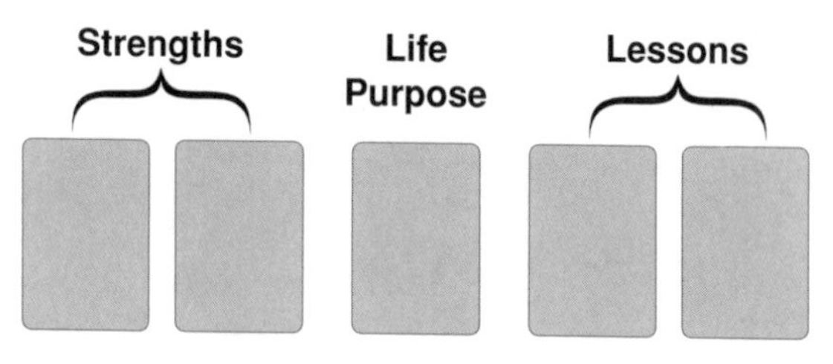

Focus on your desire to learn what your life is about. What are you to do in your life? What is your purpose here? Then, shuffle the cards. Without looking at the colors, pick five cards. Lay them out from left to right. Now turn the cards over.

The two cards on the left represent the strengths you have developed toward your life purpose. The card in the middle represents the general direction of this purpose. The two cards on the right indicate what lessons you are still learning in order to empower your life purpose. In time, the lesson cards may become the strength cards. As you master the lessons, you have created inner strength.

Read about the first card on the left by turning to its color in the ColorCards™ book. Because it has been placed in the "strength" position, read what is said about the "strengths" of this color. Do the same for the next card. When you come to the middle card, turn to its color in the book. Since it fell in the position of the Life Purpose, read what is said under the "Life Purpose" section of that color. As you look up the final two cards, read what is said under "Lessons." These last two positions indicate what you are learning that will bring your life purpose more into focus.

In the back of the Colorcards™ book, you will find a sample form that you may copy, which will assist you to keep track of what you are learning. Fill in the date and color for each position. Do the exercises suggested for the "Lesson" cards. Consider what you have learned through this card arrangement. Write about what you have learned, how you feel, and any other thoughts that come to mind. Review these sheets from time to time to monitor your progress toward your life purpose.

Understanding Situations in Your Life

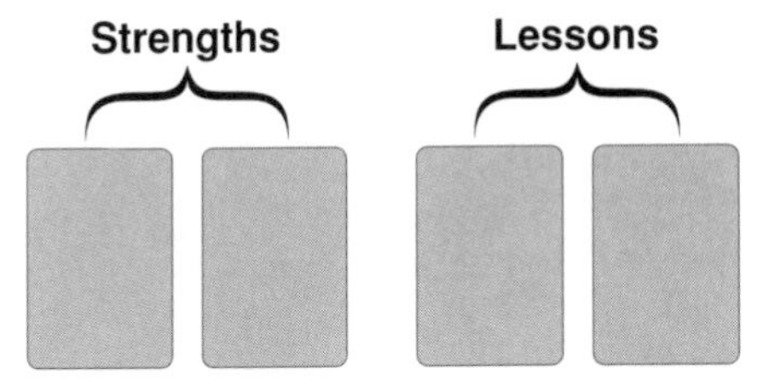

Every day, we experience situations in our lives that cause us to wonder. Why me? What does this mean? The Colorcards™ can help you understand and learn from these situations. Focus on the situation you have in mind. Be open to learning from this situation. Shuffle the cards. Without looking at the colors, choose four cards. Lay these cards out in front of you from left to right. Turn the cards over. The two cards on the left reveal the strengths you bring to this situation. Find these colors in the ColorCards™ book. Read about the strengths of these colors. The two cards on the right indicate the lessons you are learning from this situation. After finding these colors in the ColorCards™ book, read what is said about their lessons. Experience the exercises associated with these lessons. Using the form found in the back of the book, write out your feelings and new understandings. Use this newly acquired information as you continue to make your way through the situation you have focused upon.

Working with Balance in Your Life

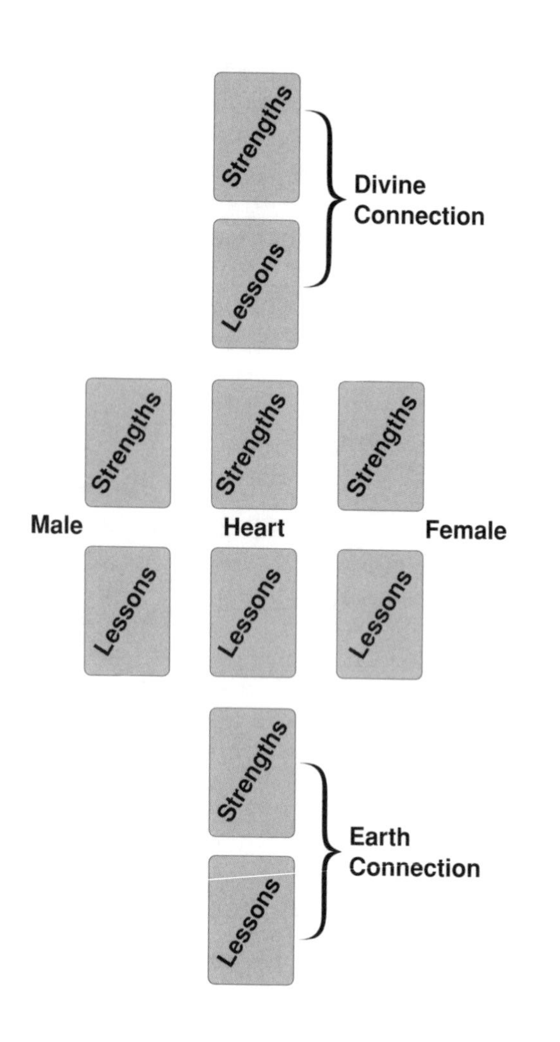

This is a more involved way of looking at your life. It

uses most of the colors in the Colorcards™ deck. You will need to use your understanding of the color and your intuition to decipher the meaning of each color by its position in the arrangement.

You are in the process of achieving balance in your life. In order to rediscover your wholeness you need a strong and clear connection with both the divine and human in your life. This means you are fully committed to your connection to the heavens and the earth. As a human being you contain within you both male and female aspects. Physically you are either male or female, but inside you work with both the female and the male ways of dealing with life. Balancing the male and female brings great empowerment. Like the Tao symbol, you are yin and yang energies working as a whole.

In order to better understand how this works, I will outline for you what I feel we are working toward in each of these areas. What I suggest is a place to begin. Trust your own understanding of this process. You may find that you differ with my interpretation or that you add to what I have said. Allow whatever has importance for you to lead you.

Our heart center brings together all the aspects of the self. This is the place of integration and wholeness. Everything about us comes together in the heart. When the heart is broken, tarnished, or hurting, it is very difficult to feel peace in our lives. Clearing and healing the heart is of prime importance.

Our connection with the heavens helps us remember that we are spiritual beings having a human experience. When we enter this life, a kind of veil is drawn so that we feel separate from who we are as spiritual beings. This is so that we may more easily focus on the learning experiences here on the earth. In order to be balanced, we must draw back the veil by claiming our divine connection. Bringing balance to our connection to the divine is a process. Experiences in our lives may have led us to distrust or to close off this connection. In this layout, you will understand more fully how to open up this divine connection. When this connection is strong, you will know who you are as a both human and divine. You will feel the expansiveness of being part of a design that is much bigger than what your human self realizes. You will know that you are loved and supported by the universe through a power that is beyond human comprehension.

Our connection with the earth is of equal importance. If we have only a divine connection, we are floating above ourselves, never fully involved. We came here for a reason. To learn what we came to learn and to do what we came to do, we must be present fully. At its best, this connection with the earth feels supportive and nurturing. We feel safe here. We experience life fully through the senses and the clarity of our minds. We are able to function easily and with confidence.

The female side of us (whether we are male or female physically) allows us to receive all that life offers. She is open, trusting, and allowing. The female aspect of us trusts her intuition. She feels the right timing in life-when to stand still, when to act, when to listen, when to speak. She cares for the self through understanding and nurturing. She births and creates the thought for whatever we wish to bring into form. She affirms our feelings and shares our pain without taking on the pain herself. She feels very connected to the earth.

The male side of us (whether we are male or female physically) acts. He sees what needs to be done and does it without judgment or coercion. He understands the larger plan for our lives. He wraps us in a protective layer of unconditional love so that we may move forward in confidence. He values clarity of mind and steadfastness of purpose. He brings things into form by creating the working blueprint for the ideas the female is birthing. He is very connected to the vastness of the universe and to that Divine Mind from which we come.

As you work with the arrangement of cards on the

next page, go back to this outline of the ideal connections. Think about the meaning of the card as it relates to that part of the self.

Each position consists of two cards. The upper card is the strength you have developed in that position. The card below it indicates the lesson you are learning in that position. For example, the upper card in the heart position indicates heart strength; the card below it indicates a heart lesson. For the color that lands in the strength location, read about the strength for that color. For the color that lands in the lesson location, read about the lesson for that color.

Focus your attention on your desire to understand your life more fully. Clearly intend that the information you receive will be exactly what you need right now in your life. Shuffle the cards. Without looking at the colors, place two cards, one above the other, in the center of the arrangement. Then place two more cards above the middle cards, then two below the middle cards, then two to the left side of the middle cards, and finally, two more to the right of the middle cards. (Follow the illustration above.) Imagine that the cards represent you standing in front of yourself. In this arrangement, the middle cards tell you about your heart, the cards above the heart indicate the state of your divine connection; the cards below the heart indicate how you are relating to the earth; the cards to the left of the heart (the right side of the body) show you what is happening with your male self; and the cards to the right of the heart (the left side of the body) indicate the status of your female self.

Use the form in the back of the book to track the colors in each of the positions. Write about what you have learned from this arrangement.

Black

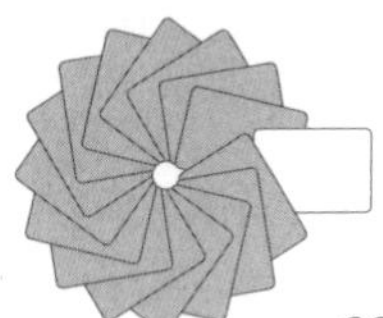

Black contains all the colors of the pigments. Its power comes from the containment of these colors. It is rich, full, focused, and beautiful. White becomes black's balance, but not in the same way as other colors. Black becomes the foundation, or platform, from which we live our lives, while white becomes the activating divine force that expands our awareness so that we experience all life as sacred. Black and white represent the duality, which is key to our existence here.

Strengths

All Possibilities are Present

Don't be put off by black. It is one of the richest colors available to you. If you mix all the pigment colors together, you will create black. This means that every color is available through black. Every possibility is potentially available to you through this color. Your strength is that you are open to the smorgasbord of possibilities. You do not close yourself off from what you can receive and learn. You are not afraid to see and experience what is presented to you.

Learning

Your strength lies in your willingness to learn. You are willing to give yourself the time and space to learn from whatever is presented to you. You do not avoid, back away from, or discount what comes to you even if it is something new. You may have been pushed to your very limit. By facing your fears and pushing through your limitations, you have developed courage, will, perseverance, and clarity.

Transformation

Black indicates your willingness to experience transformation. You may fear emotional pain and try to avoid it at all costs, yet sometimes it is the means to your transformation. Low points in life can teach you what life is all about.

Shadow Side

You are willing to look at your shadow side. This is the part of you that you may want to hide from yourself and others. This can be the part of you that speaks without thinking or acts in ways that are not consistent with who you are. It may also be the part of you that has exceptional abilities. Using those abilities might mean that you have to take on new responsibilities. You have been willing to be open and honest with yourself. You have come to accept all sides of yourself, including those you might prefer to hide. By bringing your shadow into the light, you may find that it is strength in disguise.

Focus and Hard Work

Because you are willing to face whatever comes, you are able to focus on what you need to do. You are not afraid to put your complete effort into change. This focus of energy allows you to move forward at a rapid pace.

Power

Black is powerful. Determination and focused direction create an inner power. With openness to all possibilities, the willingness to do whatever it takes to move forward, and the use of pure intention, you concentrate your energy in a purposeful direction.

Very Present

Your strength lies in your willingness to be fully

present and conscious. Avoidance is not your way. You are very present in your body and ready for action.

Life in Stages

You understand that what you are experiencing at this moment will pass. You see life in stages. Your willingness to be totally present in a particular stage of life allows you to extract its juiciness and its direction for your life.

Magic

Because you are open to all the possibilities, you may take on a magical quality that is very attractive to others. They don't always know what to expect from you. You are not totally predictable. You are not afraid to change your direction if that seems the best course. You are not opposed to investigating different parts of yourself. You seem to make things happen, even against great odds. Others may stand back to watch, because they are fascinated by the intensity and focus you exude. They may not be willing to try out what you are willing to experience, but they live through you vicariously.

Lessons

Black presents powerful lessons. It is easy to get caught in the darkness. It is not always easy to remember to ask for help. Remember that black brings great transformation and the possibility of wholeness.

Time of Transformation

One of black's biggest lessons is to know that you are in the midst of inner change. When black shows up, you are being told that you are in transition. The lesson is to accept this transformation as a positive force in your life. Don't ignore, resist, or deny this change. Bring that which needs to change into the light. See it clearly. Understand it completely. Assist yourself to change.

Too Many Choices

Because all colors are available in black, indecision may result. Your lesson is to be open to the possibilities, but to focus your direction.

Understanding Duality

The lesson in black may be to accept the world with all of its dualities. You see your life as good or bad, white or black, up or down, positive or negative. These are your everyday dualities. Accepting that you are to experience all sides of life with understanding and learning is not easy. You may have lived lives where you have been the perpetrator and lives where you have been the victim. In this life or another, you have likely experienced it all. When you see the imbalance in others, it is not your job to punish the one who is acting out a lesson of power. Instead, because you too have used power to manipulate others, you can see clearly what the person is doing. You may need to set boundaries that include removing that person from society, yet all the while, you are called to stay centered in your acceptance of the path through which each has chosen to learn. You are challenged to remember that this life is about learning from duality. By avoiding judgment and punishment of that person, you keep from becoming like him or her. You then have the opportunity to consciously choose the kind of life you live. You do this by accepting the lesson, moving through the experience, and coming out with a greater awareness and greater strength.

Fear

Fear can be debilitating. Fear of the unknown, fear of another's power, distrust of your abilities, fear of how you will use your power, fear that you will disappear or be discounted—all of these fears can keep you stuck. When something is chasing you in a dream, if you turn and face whatever it is, you find that it is not nearly as scary as you thought. The lesson in black is to face your fears. Own up to the fear that plagues you. See it for what it is. Learn about yourself through it. Seek out help from within yourself and outside of yourself. Take charge of your life. Take the reins. Forge your direction through your strength.

Protection

When you live by fear, you seek out protection. This can lead to a pulling in and shutting out. Have you created a protection around you that keeps others from knowing you? Are you keeping others at a distance? Are you protecting yourself from knowing who you are? Black teaches you that there are other ways to feel safe rather than shutting yourself off from those around you. Ask for angelic protection. Call on Divine Love. Love banishes fear. Allow yourself to know how much you are loved. Embrace that scared little child inside of you. Call on the capable part of yourself to take over. Let that little one inside you know what it feels like to be taken care of. Let it hand off that backpack of heavy responsibility it has been carrying.

Power

When you feel inadequate and uncertain of anything in your life, there is a tendency to try to control your life and everyone in it. This control can be subtle or blatant. It may appear as a need to have everything in its place. If someone moves something out of its place, you become uneasy. It may appear as a desire to know everything about a new situation—who will be there, how to get there, what will be expected of you. Children, animals, a spouse, employees all become prime targets for anger as you try to keep everything under control. There is a part of you that wants everyone to obey. Others develop resentment toward you. They either argue with you, go silent, disappear within themselves, or they leave. The lesson in black is to release control and move into trust. This can only happen when the fearful child in you knows that it is not alone. Only when you have gathered in that part of you that fears and then, have turned to solidify your divine connection can you release control and turn again toward trust. Ask your inner guidance for help to do this.

Denying the Shadow

There is a part of you that you like to keep in the shadow. You are ashamed or fearful of this part of yourself. You want to hide it away from others and yourself. In order to avoid seeing this dark side of yourself, you tend to blame others for your shortcomings or your misdeeds, or you judge others with similar shadow sides. Black teaches you to bring your shadow side into the light. Face this part of yourself. Understand it, embrace it, and heal it. Only then can you accept all of yourself. Only then can you stand fully in the light.

Selling the Soul

At its most extreme, black indicates that you have sold out. You have allowed others, or something within you, to control you to the point that you no longer have an authentic form of your own. You have lost touch with your essence. This can lead to the "dark night of the soul." When you experience this kind of darkness, you are in despair. Nothing seems worthwhile, not even life itself. Black's lesson is to reclaim you. In most cases, you will need help to do this. Asking for help is a courageous act. It means that you are ready to be honest with yourself and others. It means you are ready to face your shadow so that you can be all you are meant to be.

Removing Others' Choice

Another extreme manifestation of black is using spiritual powers as a way to have power over others. There is a fascination with this kind of power. Charisma, when it is used in order to have power over others who are vulnerable, is a kind of black magic. Creating potions to control another person is a way of using intent for power over another. The earth is a place of choice. We are required to choose for ourselves. When someone attempts to remove choice from others through manipulation, deceit, or control, this goes against the laws of the universe. This can lead to an intense time of learning, as it often draws to the person the consequences of betrayal. When these consequences follow us into another lifetime, they may be seen as karmic consequences. If you have dabbled in black magic or you have succumbed to the fascination of having power over others, black teaches you to stop. Come back to your soul center. Reclaim the divine power within you. Learn what it is to live fully in the light. Show the human part of yourself the power available when you allow the divine direction within you to lead the way. This kind of power uplifts, strengthens, and empowers you and others.

Healing Exercise

Imagine that you are in a safe place. Invite your guardian angel or some spiritual figure to join you there. When you feel completely comfortable, ask your shadow side to come to this place. When it arrives, ask it to tell you about itself. Why has it chosen to be black? What has it come to teach you? Have it show you all the possibilities that it brings you. Ask if it would be willing to help you by shifting into another color. Notice what happens. If it changes into another color, consider what that means. Write about what you have learned from this experience.

Life Purpose

Looking at All the Possibilities

You may find that you bring an expanded view to all that you do. You are not satisfied to look at only one way of doing things. You know there are many ways to meet a challenge and many ways to bring about the best conclusion to a situation. You will push yourself and others to expand their horizons and to consider all the possibilities. This may require you to take the worst of situations and turn them around by finding the underlying positives.

Accepting Duality.

Your life purpose may include showing others how to live in the duality of life. You have come to understand that we are in this life to learn. This is not a bad thing. Instead of living in judgment of the duality, you may be able to help others see the duality as a way to understand the human situation and learn about themselves.

Bringing the Shadow to Light

Because you have been willing to face your own shadow side, you will help others to face the shadow within them. These persons may go through their lessons faster than you did because you are there to help them. Sometimes, this may take you into hidden places within the person that need to experience the light. Sometimes, this may mean you must face the shadow side of society. You have learned that whether something is dark or light, it is energy that ultimately comes from the Divine Source. Therefore, within that which seems dark, there is light. You help others search for that light within the darkness. Because you have come through so much that was difficult within your own life, you know how to navigate through the obstructions. You will know how and when to ask for assistance.

Opposing the Shadow

Because you have been willing to face that which desires to stay hidden within yourself and society, you may be drawn to opposing or exposing fear, corrupted power, manipulation, or lack of integrity. Do not use tactics that breed what you oppose. Bring light into the darkness through clarity and compassion. Setting clear boundaries, exposing motivations, and showing how fear controls others may be part of your work. Because you have experienced this yourself, you know how seductive this power can be. You recognize how it works. Clarity, not force, gives others the opportunity to make their choices. It is not your place to choose for others. Your job is to shine light into dark places.

Blue

The essence of blue brings creative divine thought into form. Blue creates a blueprint, which holds material in form on the earth. This is a natural, flowing process. Blue emanates from an energy center located near the Adam's apple called the throat chakra.

The color that balances blue is orange. Orange comes from an energy center located near the navel. Orange allows you to feel your feelings through all your senses. Orange teaches you to find warmth and joy, while blue teaches you to flow. Both of these colors contain creativity within them. Orange creates through the human senses working with sight, sound, touch, smell, and taste. Blue creates through spiritual concepts (the divine blueprint) that are expressed in words, music, art, sculpture and the like.

Strengths

Blueprint

All things are essentially energy. In order for things to take form in human manifestation, there must be a blueprint that holds that form. Around the body is a blue mesh that determines the body's shape. This can sometimes be seen when you are in a deep state of meditation or just on the edge of a deep sleep. This blue mesh holds the form for this body. Your strength in blue allows you to bring things creatively into form. Your creativity may take many forms, from written and spoken words to music and art. When you bring things into form through blue, they come from your true essence, from the spiritual source within you. Sometimes, they seem to come through you from someplace beyond you.

Speaking the Truth

The color blue is understood to be located in the body at the throat; therefore, it deals with speaking. Your strength in the blue is to speak the truth in love. Your words can lift others' spirits. Your truth can set boundaries or challenge what you experience as untruth. It takes courage to speak out when others would choose to be quiet. It takes clarity to see your truth when others would persuade you otherwise. Because you are aware that you see life through your own eyes, your strength in blue allows you to know that your truth may not be another's truth. You have learned that you can follow your own truth while respecting the differences in others.

Clarity

You are likely to speak clearly, going to the heart of the matter easily. Others may be surprised how well you hear their ideas and how clearly you articulate what you hear. They value your clarity and ability to penetrate an idea to its core.

Integrity

A strength found in blue is integrity. Staying true to yourself in all things means that you do not compromise what you value. You know that others may not understand integrity in the same way you do, but you know you must stay close to your own authentic self. This means that you do not hide who you are nor do you hide behind someone else. You stand tall and clear.

Commitment

You are not afraid to make a commitment to yourself or others. You do not promise what you cannot deliver.

Loyalty

You are "true blue." You stand with those you trust,

even when they are going through difficult times. You accept them in the midst of their triumphs, and in the midst of their time of learning.

Leadership

All the strengths in blue come together to create a much-sought-after leader. Your strength lies in leading from the depth of the soul. You stand tall in the crowd because you are willing to be authentic. You are not afraid to be who you are. You have nothing to hide. You accept yourself without exception. You look for the same strengths in those who are drawn to you. You are not afraid to include others in decision-making. You are willing to be responsible for the decisions you make.

Calm and Flow

Your strength lies in your ability to flow and stay calm in all circumstances. You do not need to control situations. You have learned to move **with,** not **against,** life. Rather than force what happens in your life, you allow life to flow like a river with a sense that all is well. There is a quiet strength in this. Worry is left behind. In its place is a knowing about life. From this calm center, you experience the synchronicity of events, often finding that you are in the right place at the right time without having to plan such connections.

Affection

Those around you feel your acceptance. You do not require them to be a certain way in order to be accepted. They feel as if they are being embraced, as they are.

Inner Peace

Because you are gentle with yourself and others, you exude an inner peace that affects those around you. If they are frantic, they become calmer. If they are worried, they relax.

Expansion

There is a knowing about life that comes from within you. This allows you to expand your awareness to consider new ideas and new experiences. There is no fear of what is new or different in your calm center, only peace, curiosity, and acceptance.

Lessons

Blue is located in the throat chakra. When this energy center is closed, you close off your ability to express yourself in whatever form might be appropriate. You cannot create a blueprint for what you desire when this part of you is blocked.

Speaking Up

Blue teaches you to speak up. As a child, you may have learned that it was dangerous to speak out and express your ideas and feelings. You have been holding back, not saying what needs to be said. You may feel that you will be punished if you speak out. You may feel that you will be laughed at or made fun of if you express what you are feeling. You may be afraid that your words will hurt someone. These words start deep in your belly with the emotions that are behind them. Bring the unexpressed emotions up through your heart and out your throat. Allow yourself to know the perfect timing and the perfect way for these words to be said. Sometimes talking to yourself or writing out what you want to say relieves the pressure that has built up. When you speak, speak from the heart. Speak with clarity, without finding fault or blaming. Speak about what you are feeling, what you have experienced, and what you need. Avoid saying "you" or "should." Speak from the heart, using "I feel . . . I need . . . I experience . . ."

Communication

Your lesson is to learn to communicate in a clear, authentic, caring way. This may require that you tap into your **desire** to communicate, your **courage** to begin, and your **willingness** to learn from your mistakes. The longer you put off this lesson, the more you will experience miscommunication, which can lead to difficulties in your job, your family, and your relationships. You may find that you are forced to communicate with the most difficult person in your life in order to break through the dam you have allowed or created. Accept the lesson now so that you may come into a time of easy, clear, open communication that brings all your relationships into a new perspective.

Leadership

Blue draws you into leadership. Your lesson in this arena is to stay close to your inner truth. Your ability to lead others can be seductive. Don't lose sight of the deeper purpose. Being swept away by your own ability to draw others to you can stifle the flow.

Creating from the Soul

Deep within you is something that needs to be expressed creatively. It comes from a place that is soul deep. To deny it means that you are denying the expression of who you are and what your life is about. This denial can lead to an ache in the throat and an ache in the soul. It is time to discover what is blocking this deep desire to create.

Isolation

Too much blue can cause you to be isolated. You may have closed yourself off from people, experiences, or even yourself. Others may feel as if the real part of you is frozen in a piece of ice. They seem unable to penetrate to the real you. The lesson in blue is to discover the fears that have closed you down and shut you out. You may feel like you are lost in a blue fog, not knowing how to reconnect. Stop the emotions, the thoughts, the "what if's," long enough to ask for help. Breathe in and out. Ask your inner self for help, ask those unseen guides for help, ask that Divine Parent of the universe for help. Pay attention to the answers. They may come from the most unexpected places.

Depression

When you close down communication and creativity, you may sink into a deep well of depression. You may feel there is no way out. You may be looking through the eyes of a child part of you that feels all alone. You will not find the answers from the child's perspective. You will need to shift into that capable part of yourself that sees a bigger picture than the child. This may not be an easy process. You may need help to balance your body, mind, and spirit. Seek out the correct practitioners to assist you. Once your balance begins to be restored, you can then hold that child inside of you, letting it know it is not alone. You can bring it into your heart to be held and nurtured. Let that inner child receive all the love you can extend. Choose to be with others who are positive and affirming as you go through this process.

Manifesting

You have a great ability to bring things into form, or you would not be blocking the blue color. So long as you allow the blockage to persist, you will experience lack in many parts of your life. Are you ready for the abundance that is yours? Are you ready to receive even more than you need in all areas of your life? Allow blue to flow, so that your abundance may flow also.

Flow

Have you been running your life like a machine? Have you been pushing yourself to your limits? Blue encourages you to let go and trust your heart, which knows the bigger picture and can create flow in your life. Blue may be telling you that it is time to be quiet, to allow life to flow in a soothing pattern. Perhaps you need rest and relaxation, time to be alone, time to heal, and time to know yourself more deeply. Are you taking care of your body? Are you listening to your needs? Are you allowing others to do their part? Are you limiting what you are doing so that you can truly accomplish all that you have set before yourself? Flow can only occur when you allow it into your life. By using your intention, decide now to take care of yourself. Intend to bring a peaceful flow into your life.

Healing Exercise

Close your eyes and imagine you see a beautiful blue sky. Allow yourself to become part of the blue. Feel yourself expand into the sky and beyond into the universe. Feel and know that you are part of a huge world that is much more than what you experience day to day. Be healed by the soothing color blue. After a while you notice that the sun is setting on the horizon. Streaks of orange penetrate the blue. Move into the orange. Feel its tenderness and warmth. Allow yourself to feel completely, using all your senses. Allow yourself to be held in this warmth and comfort for as long as you wish. Notice how you can flow with the blue while experiencing a core of orange glow. As you return to this time and space, maintain this flow and inner glow. Let yourself speak inwardly of all you have bottled up inside. Feel all that you have been afraid to feel. Write freely in your journal. Say all of what you have been afraid to speak about. If you ask your heart, which contains your truth, you will know what to do with what you have written.

Life Purpose

Creative expression

Blue indicates that you have creative talent. As you express what you feel so deeply, you may find that the form this expression takes may vary. You may be an author, artist, architect, actor, politician, or you may prefer some other form of expression. Your purpose is to bring things into form from your inner truth. Others will benefit from what you express.

Soothing Presence

Part of your purpose may be to bring a soothing, healing presence into places of confusion, anger, and hurt. Look for all the places in your life where this is needed. As you bring that inner flow into your own life, you will be showing others how to do the same. You will need times of quiet contemplation, times to journal and find your calm center, so that your presence continues to be soothing and whole.

Speaking Out

Your life purpose may push you to speak out when others choose to be silent. This may not be easy. Blue encourages you to persevere, for this is your path. Learn to bring your words from a calm center. Allow that others may disagree and this is their right. Call on your inner guidance. Draw strength from your friends. Detach from the outcome. Allow the Universal Intelligence to guide the process and the result.

Leadership

You are meant to be a leader. Others sense that you

can bring whatever you envision into form. Because they know that you feel this from the depth of your soul, they will follow you as it manifests. Be sure that you stay true to yourself as you lead others. Listen, consider, and allow others to contribute.

Brown

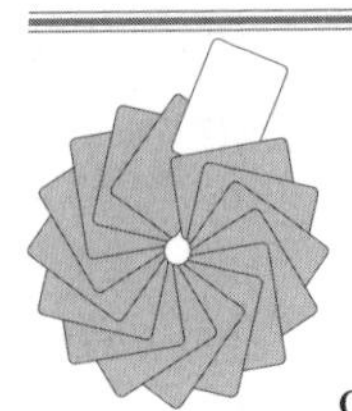

Brown is of the earth. It is made up of yellow, orange and green: yellow for the warmth of the sun, orange for the depth of emotion and aliveness through the senses, and green for growth and healing. Brown's balancing color is a muted blue of a dusty sky. Like a mother, brown gathers her creatures to her, holding them close, yet not too close, so that they may learn from their time on Earth. Her simple warmth and caring heal old wounds and reestablish trust. She is fertile, birthing life abundantly.

Strengths

Nurturing

Your love is never pushy or overbearing. You are present and ready to serve others as you are needed. You seem to know the need before you are asked. Others feel as if they have been gathered into the arms of the Great Mother. Here they feel safe, accepted, and cared for.

Safety

You feel safe on the earth. You help others to feel safe here, too. This allows the healing to begin. Children, and the child in each person, may be drawn to you, because they know you will hold them close with great love and compassion.

Connection to the Earth

You are at home on the earth. You know how to receive nurturance and sustenance from the earth. You become one with the trees, flowers, animals, rocks—all the earth has to offer. Earth's bounty feeds not only your body, but also your soul. Working in the yard or garden, walking in the woods, along the seashore, or through the desert, you feel at home. The various smells, textures, and colors of the earth soothe you. Wriggling your toes in the earth brings you simple pleasure.

Growth

For you, life is about birthing, nurturing, and growing. From seed to flowering plant, you water, cultivate, and nurture living things into maturity. You support and encourage others' to grow, move ahead, and become all that they can be.

Stability

Feeling at home on the earth gives you stability from which to live your life. Connecting yourself to the center of the earth gives you strength It would take a great deal to push you away from your center or break that connection.

Simplicity and Sharing

Your needs are simple. You desire only what you need at this moment. You know you receive all that you need and more. You feel richly blessed. Every day is a day to give thanks. You share this abundant harvest with others.

Feeling Deeply

Because you are so connected to your body, you feel through all your senses. You feel what others feel as well. You are open to all of these feelings, knowing that what you experience does not need to overwhelm you. The earth will "recycle" any emotions that you are ready to release.

Connecting to the Body

Living in the body is natural to you. The fewer clothes you need to wear, the better. You love walking barefooted. Your body is relaxed, open, and swings naturally to an inner rhythm. You accept your body as beautiful no matter how it measures up to the standards of the world. You take good care of your body through proper nourishment, exercise, and rest. You make love with your whole body, expressing deep emotional caring.

Sound and Movement

The sound of drums is the heartbeat of the earth. Low, rich, and resonating, the drums echo the sounds of the earth. Dancing to the beat of the drums comes naturally to you. Your movement is flowing, rhythmic, and sensual, like the energy that flows through the earth.

Laughter

Your laughter is hearty, coming from deep within the body. You delight in the comical antics of all living beings. You find humor in humans' preoccupation with the complexities in life. For you, life is simple, free, and without encumbrance.

Honesty

There is no pretense in you. You are straightforward. What you present is who you are. What you say is what you mean.

Lessons

Brown, by itself, can be overburdened much like Earth is. If you take on all the emotions and pain that others are experiencing, or if you try to nurture and heal everyone around, you will find that you have nothing left. The lesson in brown is to balance Earth and Heaven, human and divine. Then, all things are possible.

Smothering

Because you have not been mothered enough yourself, the great mothering instinct in you tries to make everyone around you feel safe and cared for. You have become adept at knowing exactly what others need. You want to heal their suffering. The danger is that you will smother others by holding them too close. You cannot do for them what they must do for themselves. Suffering may be their wake-up call to healing. Don't sidetrack them by your own need for their suffering to cease. You can still love them and be there for them, as they need you. Instead, turn your mothering in upon yourself. Hold close that child within you that cries out for your great embrace.

Avoidance of Suffering

Because you feel things so deeply, there may be a tendency to float above the suffering you feel around you. Without the stability and nurturance from being planted firmly on the earth, you will be unable to be present in your life. You will be unable to do what you came here to do, to help in the way you want to. Bring yourself into the moment. Be courageous enough to be fully present. Allow the earth to help you feel safe.

Losing your Life Force

Because others are drawn to your strength and healing, you may feel your life force being sucked from you. Show them how to find the light within them. Remember your need for solitude and simplicity. Spend time in nature. Replenish your resources. Care for yourself and your needs so that you may be present for others.

Giving Can Be Taking

Because there are so many unmet needs within you, your giving may feel like taking. You may not realize that through your attempts to heal and care for others, you are filling your own needs. In fact, your attempt to heal others may actually be draining the life force from them. You may also be holding others back because you want to hold on to them. You want them to need you. First, fill your own inner needs. Heal what needs to be healed within you. Then, you will be able to help others in a caring, yet more detached, way.

Bound by the Earth

Because you feel so attached to the earth, you may find that you see and experience only the human perspective. You may become caught up in the drama here. Without that broader spiritual connection, you limit your experience; you narrow your focus; you get lost in the earth-drama. You may even participate in creating more drama through negativity, blame, and judgment. Move through the earth to the moon. Allow it to lighten and enlighten your path. Remember the great plan you have come to be part of. Stay close to the earth, but broaden your perspective to encompass all of who you are.

Humiliation

Brown's lesson may be for you to recognize the humiliation you have suffered in your life. You may have felt like you never measured up to the standards set before you. You may feel you are not worthy of love. You may feel that you are less than others. Like the peasants of the past who wore brown instead of the bright colors of the aristocracy, you may be wearing brown in your aura, seeing your station in life as lower than others. Own up to who you are! You are a magnificent being living in human clothing. The humiliation you have felt can be your wake-up call. You can see your sense of lowliness for what it is. The persons who humiliated you do not feel good about themselves. Their need to make you less than them came from their own misunderstanding of themselves, their own insecurities and lack of inner respect. Wake up! Learn who you truly are. Be grateful for your abilities, your inner gifts, and your loving presence. You have so much to give yourself and others. Now is the time to reclaim who you are!

Lack of Trust

If your connection to the earth is superficial, you will feel that there is never enough of anything to go around. You will expect lack in all parts of your life. You will feel a need to hold on to what you have for fear that you won't get your share. You will feel that you are never taken care of. You will not trust what life offers you. You will withhold what you have from yourself and others. What a pitiful way to live! Open up to the bounty that is yours. There is enough to go around. You have only to respect the earth, work with it instead of against it, ask for what you need, and then allow yourself to receive. However, if you take back the reins because you don't believe there is any help, the universe will allow you to go forward on your own. Your attitude can create your reality. Your need to learn a lesson in trust can create experiences of lack. See it for what it is. This is an opportunity to feel your connection to the bounty of the universe. Allow yourself to trust in small ways. Notice the results. Move forward a step at a time until you have experienced the way of trust so often that it becomes a way of life.

Obsession with Self

Living in distrust leads to self-absorption. If you feel there is no help available, that you are alone here, that everyone cares only for himself or herself, you will spend all of your time looking out for yourself. Your focus will be so tightly drawn around you that you will not even notice how you have shut others out. Loneliness will be the result. Just a step away is all that you need. Connect to Mother Earth; feel how she cares for you, nurtures you, holds you in her loving arms. Notice the beauty that is around you. Feel the joy of the birds singing, the warmth that the sun offers. Ask for help when you need it. Draw into that divine connection that lives in the center of your heart. Open your arms to that great love that emanates from beyond. You are not alone.

Feeling Stuck

Do you feel like you are walking through deep mud? Is every step difficult, every move forward full of pain? Brown may be teaching you to stop. Look into yourself to see what you are avoiding. What have you been unwilling to look at within yourself? What do you fear? Ask yourself why everything seems so difficult. Ask the pain to show you what you need to face within yourself. Feel the mud; wriggle your toes in it. Don't blame it for holding you back. Learn this lesson so you may move on.

Dishonesty

Because you do not feel safe, you feel you must not tell all you know. You fit the truth to what you think others want to hear. You hold back anything that you are not sure about. You weigh your words carefully to see if they can be taken in a way that will make others angry or cause you discomfort. Only when you have come to a comfortable place inside yourself can you speak openly and honestly. Only then will others trust what you say and do.

Healing Exercise

Take time to connect with the earth. Take long walks in the woods or along a stream. Listen to the sounds of the earth. Notice the beauty it offers. Take off your shoes and dig your toes into the ground. Sit in quietness. Feel yourself anchored deep into the earth. Give thanks for this creation of such variety, beauty, and love.

Life Purpose

Love of the Earth

Your life purpose may be to connect so deeply with the earth that you feel you are part of it. You will then feel oneness with trees, flowers, birds, animals, rocks, everything of the earth. Your love for the earth will fill up your heart. As you extend this energy of love to the earth, you will help to heal it. Your deep sense of gratitude for the earth is a prayer that extends to the center of all creation.

Healing the Earth

You may feel drawn to playing an active part in healing the earth. You may participate in groups that seek to save the vegetation and creatures of the earth. You may become part of the leadership of such a group. This may lead to educational campaigns or political action nationally or internationally.

Appreciating the Earth

You may be drawn to helping others appreciate Earth's beauty and strength. This may come through art, music, drumming, lectures, poetry, or some other means. Whatever the medium, communicating your love for the earth will be important to you.

Receiving from the Earth

Teaching others how to connect with the earth, how to gain nourishment from the earth, or how to use the healing energy of the earth to bring wholeness to themselves and others may all be part of your path. The earth has so much to offer. Her bounty is endless so long as we care for her.

Healing the Inner Child

Your life purpose in brown may be to teach others how to bring comfort and love to their inner child. First, you will learn to care for that child within you. Then, you will be prepared to help others.

Teaching Children

Because you create a sense of safety and warmth, children will be drawn to you. This may lead you to teaching or nurturing children in some way.

Appreciating the Body

Your life purpose may lead you to help others appreciate their bodies. This may be through dance or movement, working in a spa to pamper the body, teaching sensuous living, or many other possibilities for keeping the body healthy and beautiful.

Natural Remedies

You may be drawn to alternative medicine and remedies that come from nature, such as herbs and aromatherapy. This could be as a healing practitioner or a teacher. Other remedies might include building homes that express a natural architecture or music that heals. Colors taken from the earth might be used in art or healing techniques. Whatever Mother Nature has to offer can be used to uplift and heal.

Gold

Gold is a very high vibration. Its warmth and vibrancy can raise you to a place of grateful acceptance of who you are.

Like black and white, gold and silver are part of the duality. They are not so much a balance for each other as they are a completion of each other. Bring gold and silver into your body and your aura as one penetrating light. When you are comfortable working with both gold and silver, you are working with high vibrations of male and female energy.

Gold and silver can also be used with other colors. For example, on the inside of your egg-shaped energy field call an aura, visualize blue to hold the shape of the aura, and on the outside of the aura-shell visualize gold and silver to create an outer lining that will contain your energy and refine other energies before they reach you.

Strengths

Value

Gold is given great value in our world. It is hidden away until it is found and mined. Not everyone owns gold, so it is considered rare, something that everyone wishes to possess. When gold is your strength, you are valued highly. You will be sought out for your leadership and abilities. You bring a warm glow to everyone around.

Choosing What You Value

Gold's strength is in knowing what you value. Through your life experiences, you have learned to say "yes" to this and "no" to that. Your boundaries are clear. You spend your energy and time on what counts most to you. You do not give your time, money, or energy away to someone or something out of guilt or a need to please. When you give, it comes from a deep sense of caring. Your gift is wrapped in warmth. You give because you desire to give. The gift is given freely, without strings attached.

Wisdom

There is strength of clarity in yellow. Gold takes this strength to a place of wisdom born of experience. What you have experienced has taught you what to value, how to spend your time, who to connect to, and how to create balance in your life. This brilliant wisdom allows itself to be seen, but never imposes itself on others.

Connection to the Source

Gold indicates that you are solidly connected to the Divine Source. You recognize that all of life comes from the Source. Everything you do or say is affected by that connection.

Solidity

Gold indicates that your human integrity and your divine integrity are solidly in place. You stay true to yourself in all situations. You do not change like a chameleon. When you say "yes, " you mean what you say. When you say "no," you clearly mean no. You agree with others only if you truly agree. If you are put into a situation where you must stand up for what you believe, you do so without hesitation. At the same time, you do not expect others to always agree with you. You respect their values as well.

Discernment

Gold has a great strength of discernment. You see below the surface of people and situations. You know the truth even when it has not yet been revealed. You also see life from a divine perspective. You accept others in their humanness while still knowing them as the larger beings that they are. You are able to observe, accept, and understand what you see from a broader perspective.

Purification

Gold shows that you are strong within yourself. Just as gold is heated until the impurities have melted away, so you have been purified through your experiences. That which is superfluous, that which would sidetrack you from what you are here to do, that which would call you into human drama, have all been melted away. Purity of thought and action are yours.

Protection

You carry gold around you. It creates a solid lining that allows in only that which is in your highest interest. With this protective lining, you can express your spirituality openly and clearly.

Trusted Friend

Gold symbolizes the importance of relationships in your life. You have many deep friendships that last throughout life. There is a great trust between you and your friends and family. They know that you are faithful and true in all ways. You would never intentionally hurt or reject them. You will always be there in the good times and the tough times.

Warmth and Caring

Your strength is in your warmth, enthusiasm, caring, and desire to bring joy to all of life. Like the sun, you may often become the center of attention because many are attracted to your warmth and light.

Wealth

You attract wealth on all levels. Whatever you touch turns to gold. Projects you start are successful. Ideas you put forth are well received. Persons of influence look to you for wisdom and assistance. Money comes to you easily. There is a golden glow of richness that flows with you in your day-to-day existence and in your inner divine life.

Lessons

The unbalanced side of gold comes from losing the divine connection. When this happens, you fail to see your value, and your warmth and light seem diminished. It is difficult to see which way to go. The lesson in gold is to reconnect with the divine side of life. This will spin gold from threads of despair and bring back the brilliance that is always available.

Search for Purpose

Gold may be suggesting that it is time to look for the divine purpose in your life. Perhaps you have felt a void, a sense of wandering and uselessness. Gold would bring you into the light within, where you will find all the answers. That part of you deep within knows what you are to be about. You have only to ask and listen.

Solidify Life

Gold may be telling you to look for ways to solidify your life. Perhaps you have tried a number of different paths to your truth. Now is the time to find your most authentic way of life that will lead to your fulfillment.

Seeking the Warmth and Light

Gold would bring light back into your life. If you go inward and experience your life as it is, you will find that there are places of light and warmth, but putting your attention on what is not working or seeing only the negative in people and experiences may have turned off the light.

Deception

Have you been less than honest in your dealings? Have you hidden your actions from your family and friends? Gold teaches you to be done with half-truths or out-and-out lies. Allow yourself to bring all of who you are into the light. Connect even your darkest corners with the brilliance of gold. Be transformed by the golden light of truth and honesty.

Image

You have set up a false front for others to see. What they see looks like gold, but it isn't. This comes from your fear that you are not good enough to stand the true light of gold. Now is the time to be who you truly are. As you touch into that deep place of truth, you will find that you are pure spun gold. There is more within your depths than you can imagine.

Wavering Image

Another way to keep from being known is to present a wavering image—one that others cannot truly track. There is no need for this, either. Be authentic. Be true to yourself. You deserve to know how wonderful you are.

Graven Image

Because you do not trust yourself, you have looked for solidity outside of yourself. You have put your trust in others instead of knowing the truth within yourself. This will always lead to disappointment. There is gold within you. Be willing to dig for the gold to find your valuable and precious self.

Hoarding

Are you afraid you will lose what you have? Hoarding what you have limits your enjoyment of life. Whether you hold back your contribution to life or whether you hang on to your money and possessions, you limit your experiences. Release the cords that bind you. Live a life full of gratitude. The more you express your gratitude, the more you open your self to receive. The more you share yourself and your possessions out of gratitude, the more you will enjoy your life and know the returns of love and abundance.

Distrusting Wisdom

When you distrust what you know, you leave yourself open to the control of others; you allow others to be your barometer for what is right for you. By not being responsibe for your own understanding of life, you limit what you can discover and experience. Learn to access the truth that resides deep within your heart. Allow life to teach you how to work with that truth. Wisdom comes to those who are willing to go through the refining fire of life.

Hardening

The tough experiences of your life can either lead you into a deeper understanding of life or cause you to close up, become hard and unyielding. Know that each tough experience has a gift of learning within it. As you accept that gift, you gain wisdom and understanding. No one has forced this opportunity to learn upon you. You either allowed it or helped create it. Becoming hardened cannot bring you joy, peace, or safety. Only facing life squarely while calling on your inner guidance for help can take you into that place of wisdom.

Talking out of Both Sides of your Mouth

Have you told others only what they want to hear? Like a politician, you may be very adept at knowing what to say and not say. When you operate from this place of pleasing, not from integrity, you may soon have trouble knowing your own truth. You will feel like you have sold your soul. Who and what you are have been lost in striving to please others. Take time by yourself to become clear. Choose to live from this clarity in all aspects of your life. Bring the warmth and joy of gold back into your life.

Healing Exercise

On a sunny day, find a place on the beach or in a field of golden wheat, or on a sunny rock in the park. Turn yourself to the sun. Allow it to soak into your every cell. Express your gratitude for this warmth and light. Make a conscious decision to experience and appreciate all of the warmth and light that comes into your life through people, through beauty, through books you read, and through the thoughts you foster.

If there are no sunny days right now, find a quiet place where you can sit in total relaxation. Imagine the most beautiful sunny day you've ever experienced or create one in your mind's eye. Soak in what you experience just as you would if the sun were warming your face and back.

Life Purpose

Creating Places of Gold

Gold indicates that your life direction may be about creating warm, loving relationships as well as places for people to experience acceptance and caring. Sacredness and beauty will be part of all you create. Whatever you envision, you will be able to bring into form.

Leadership

You may be called to lead in some area of your life. Your integrity, wisdom, and warmth will be greatly appreciated in your leadership. Be prepared for some opposition to your light and happiness. There are many who will try to take it from you. Hold fast to what you know to be true. Your life path may take you into places where that light and your strength of character are vital.

Abundance

You are likely to experience great abundance in your life. This will include money, friends, loving relationships, and satisfying experiences. You may be showing others the way to this life of abundance as well.

Teaching Values

You have learned to value yourself and others. Now, you can show others how to choose what they value, how to live by what they value, and how to value themselves.

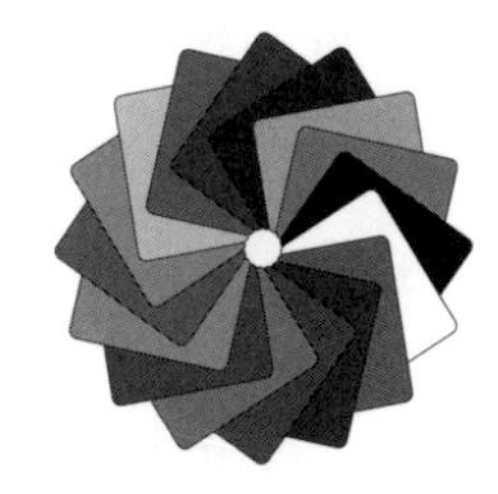

Green

The essence of green is integration, bringing together the material and spiritual aspects of life. This allows for new growth and moving ahead. The color green is located in the heart chakra. The three charkas below it relate to the earth; the three charkas above it relate to the heavens. Green becomes the conduit between the two worlds.

The balancing color for green is red. Red brings the fire to get things going. Green spurts forth in new shoots and growing edges. Red creates the foundation for the growth and healing.

Strengths

Openheartedness

Your strength lies in your willingness to open your heart. Your love pours forth from your true center. You breathe in love; then breathe out love in rhythmic waves. Those around you feel acceptance, openness, support, and caring. Your words heal and bring hope. Your actions come from compassion and understanding.

Vulnerability

Living openheartedly means that you are willing to be vulnerable. You don't need to cover up your deepest feelings. You receive back acceptance just as you have given it out.

Growth

Because you are open to all possibilities, you move ahead easily. You continually discover new parts of yourself and renew what has been on hold within you for a while. You claim what is new and cherish what is old. You are never content to say that nothing can be done to change a situation. For you, change is a natural part of life like the changing seasons. Your energy and enthusiasm are infectious. Others are caught up in your hope and sense of moving ahead.

Encouraging Change in Others

Whenever possible, you help others experience change within themselves. You encourage, affirm, and nudge them into moving ahead. You realize that whether they change or remain in stagnation, they are the ones who choose, so you do not push them. You are always available when they are ready to continue ahead.

Decisiveness

Making decisions comes easily to you because you are so connected to your center. You feel and know what is right for you. Your divine connection gives you a broader view, so that your decisions take into account all aspects of your life. You are aware of how your decisions will affect others, so, while staying true to yourself, you consider the consequences that your decisions will have on others.

Strong Connection

Green creates a strong stem that connects deep earth roots to beautiful flowers that reach to the heavens. You live within a balance of the human and the divine. You honor the body by caring for it; you honor the drama around you by understanding it; yet, you receive guidance from your deep spiritual self in all that you do. You never discount the pain you and others suffer, yet you are not immobilized by it. You recognize how the pain leads you to the learning that is available through it.

Self-Control

The integrated nature of green allows you to embrace any part of yourself that is feeling alone or out of control. That rebellious child within you feels understood and cared for. There is no need to lash out or act up.

Inclusivity

Your desire is for everyone to feel included, for everyone's abilities to be valued. Your supportive nature allows others to feel that they can join in and try out new ideas.

New Ideas

Green indicates that you relish new ideas. You like to expand them creatively as you experience them. You enjoy sharing them with others and hearing their response. This includes taking old ideas and seeing them in a new way.

Togetherness

You wish to bring your friends and family and all people together in love. It seems such a waste of life for people to be separate, angry, and uncompromising. You continuously search for ways to help them bridge the gaps and repair their relationships. Mediation is a natural ability that you bring to every situation.

Healing

Your strength lies in your natural ability to heal. Love is the basis of this healing. At times, not a word is spoken, yet the healing takes place through your heart, as empathy and caring flow through you. At other times, this healing energy flows through your hands as you touch yourself or another with love.

Love of Nature

Green draws you to it through nature. The green of the plants, the grass, and the trees all speak of the fresh, vulnerable, openhearted life force that runs through that which is alive and growing. Experiencing this life force renews and enlivens you completely.

Lessons

The unbalanced aspect of green comes when you close the heart. When the heart is closed nothing feels integrated. Everything feels separate and out of control. Change becomes scary. Being vulnerable feels dangerous. Only when the heart is open to both give and receive can the balance be restored.

Closed heartedness

When the heart is closed, it is easy to move into jealously, envy, stinginess, deceit, indecisiveness, rigidity, and even cruelty. You are out of touch with your center. Your inner child-self feels abandoned and scared. Your natural knowingness is cut off. You are unable to receive love from any direction. It is time to break this pattern. Discover why you have closed your heart. You may have been terribly wounded in your life so that it is hard to trust or open up. Listen to yourself. Seek help if necessary. Persevere in learning how to open your heart again, how to move into that inner balance and wholeness.

Broken heartedness

Your trust and vulnerability may have been trampled. Your love may have been rejected. The pain of this can feel like a broken, bleeding heart. It is easy to move into blame and a desire to punish the source of your pain. The lesson in green is to look deep within the heart. What are you to gain from this experience? If this has happened before, you may need to break a pattern that sets you up to be hurt. Have you been looking for love in all the wrong places? Have you given yourself away? Have you failed to take responsibility for your own life? Ask your broken heart. The truth is present there.

Guilt

Have you turned blame in on yourself? Have you been going over and over perceived past mistakes? It is time to set yourself free. Step across the chasm between this world and the next. See your life from the perspective you would have if you had died and were looking down at all your experiences. What was the real meaning of what you have done? What can you learn from your actions and reactions? Making mistakes is part of learning. Admitting those mistakes, learning from those mistakes, and beginning again is healthy.

Closing In

Green may be showing you that you are living out of fear. Have you closed yourself off from others? Are you afraid of anything new or different? Are you afraid to explore all the possibilities? Are you holding back for fear of ridicule? Are you shut off so you don't receive love and you don't give love? Does being vulnerable feel like self-destruction? If so, you have cut off the flow of energy from your heart. Your stem may be planted in the earth, but it will never be strong or support a flower until the flow is restored. Below the surface there is part of you that feels unprotected and alone. Only you can reclaim this part of youself and bring it into your wholeness. Let it experience the love you have for it in your heart. Let it know there is a capable part of you that can take charge. Call on the help that is available for you. You are not alone.

Unseasoned

Green may be showing you that you are unseasoned. What do you need to do to gain practical experience in life? Have you been floating off into your own world, not paying attention to what is happening here in this moment? Perhaps it is time to become conscious and aware. Look to others who seem to know the ways of the world. There is no need to become hard or suspicious, just awake and conscious.

Insincere Caring

When you need love so badly, you sometimes mold yourself to be what you think others want. Have you put on a pretense of caring in order to belong or be taken seriously? Have you given of yourself in order to keep other persons around or have them feel that they cannot do without you? If so, you have sold out on yourself. If you will open your heart, you will find what it is that you really care about. As you give yourself to that, you will naturally draw to you others who care in the same way.

Healing Exercise

Choose a day in the spring or create such a day in your imagination. Find a place where the grass is green, the trees are in full bud, and the air is crisp and alive. Breathe in the green that is all around you. Let it enliven your body and soul. Feel the movement in the growing things: sap rising, new growth moving out. Sit with your back against a tree. See if you can feel its energy. Find a rhythm internally that matches the energy of the tree. Feel the oneness of all things. Notice how rejuvenated you feel. Life is good. Express your gratitude for the gift of life.

Life Purpose

Helping Others

You may be drawn to work as a counselor, teacher, minister, or parent from your great desire to help others achieve growth and wholeness. Your deep compassion and ability to stay centered in any circumstances will be valuable in your work. As you listen to what is being said and as you help others learn from their past, you will be able to draw on your broad perspective, which includes both the human and divine aspects.

Caretaker of Nature

Your desire to allow nature to spring forth in all its beauty may lead you to work among plants and growing things as a gardener, farmer, forester or other similar job. In this work, you will feel fresh, alive, and valued for the work you do.

Mediator

Your job at home or at work may be to bring others together. You will be able to help people hear and respect each other. Your gifts include your ability to stand back and see the complete picture in any circumstance as well as your ability to accept both the humanness and the divinity in yourself and others. With these gifts, you will be able to look through others' eyes and know what they need. You will be able to articulate what you see for those who come to you for help.

Healer

You may find that healing is a natural part of your life. Whether you incorporate this into your work or simply bring it into your everyday life, you will assist others to see their lives clearly. You will help them draw on their inner courage to move forward into their own healing. You will be helping others to integrate all parts of themselves: body, mind, and spirit. Your assistance may show up in a variety of forms, from counseling to hands-on healing.

Lover of Life

Whatever you do, wherever you are, you offer openhearted love to all. You celebrate life. You gain strength from the vitality and beauty of growing things around you. This attitude helps to heal the earth and people alike. Others will be drawn into this positive, energizing force you exude.

Indigo

The deep blue/purple shade of indigo combines the ability to bring things into form with the intuitive connection that comes from deep within the self. Indigo indicates that you have likely returned to the earth many times. Indigo reaches back through all your lifetimes, gathering in knowledge and abilities you have gained from your experiences here.

The color that balances indigo is a yellow/orange. Breathe in yellow/orange; breathe out indigo. Gold may also be used with indigo to combine a deep wisdom gained from your experiences on the earth with a deep intuitive knowing that comes from the divine realm.

Strengths

Ancient Knowledge

When indigo is your strength, you are a very old soul. You have lived many lifetimes. All of what you have gained from those lifetimes is available to you as you open to this knowledge. You may have been punished for what you knew in those lifetimes, or sometimes you may have misused your power. Therefore, you may be reluctant to open to all that you know. Be assured that you can now create a strong intention to use your experience and wisdom wisely in this lifetime. Know that there may be those who will not understand what you know, but you do not need to be in physical danger in this lifetime as you exhibit these abilities.

Seeing through the Third Eye

Intuitive abilities have traditionally been understood to come through an invisible "eye" in the middle of the forehead called the "third eye." Not everyone develops this gift, and not everyone wants to develop this gift. In most cases it is a choice. In some instances, this gift is experienced early in life by knowing things or seeing things that others do not know or see, but because it is not understood, it becomes frightening. Often it is then shut down until a later time. In some persons, it is never accessed. When seeing through the third eye, you may feel as if you are looking through a different lens. Time has no meaning. You may be seeing something from the past, the present, or the future. You may be seeing forms that seem to come from another time and place. Sometimes this can be a bit confusing, because you are moving into territory that is new and different. Over time, you will learn to differentiate between what you are seeing here and now, and what you are seeing that comes from what we understand to be the past or future or from some place beyond us. You will learn to navigate between time dimensions and vibration dimensions. Sharing thoughts with someone who has died or someone from another place in the universe can be as natural as speaking to someone here on Earth. If this ability opens up too quickly for you, ask your third eye to open more slowly. Something you are wrestling with in this lifetime may be the result of experiences from another lifetime. Persons you encounter here may treat you in a certain way due to your relationship with them in another lifetime. All of this information can help you understand yourself and others more completely so that you may finish the lessons you have set out for yourself now.

Receiving and Sending Thoughts

As you develop the third eye, you may find that you perceive thoughts that come from another person, even when that person is not present. You may know things without knowing how you know. For example, you may know who is on the telephone before you pick up the receiver. Others may answer questions that come from your inner thoughts even though the thoughts have not been spoken. This ability can be used to stay alert and present in every situation. Thoughts are electrical impulses that can travel from one mind to another. Sending and receiving these impulses is a matter of tuning in to the right station. Unconsciously, you send and receive messages even in your sleep. You may also find that you are learning during your sleep or helping others as your mind and spirit travel through the universe.

Deeper Understanding

Intuition is a wonderful tool. It can warn you what to avoid. It can nudge you to act in the right timing. It can help you "see through" other people and situations. You may intuitively know that a person is lying or that what you see is not what is. You may even intuit the consequences before they happen. As you are willing to pay attention to this understanding, your life will flow more easily.

Manifestation

Through the third eye, manifesting what you envision is taken to an intuitive level. This means that the unseen help that is available to you hears your request and helps to orchestrate the results. It is important to use this tool consciously; otherwise you may manifest what you don't want. Synchronicities often result from this kind of manifesting. Your human self may be surprised how a plan takes shape or how something comes to you in perfect timing, yet your intuitive self set it up that way.

Competence

When indigo is your strength, you are seen by others as competent and able. It seems as if you have everything under control. In truth, you are simply adept at envisioning results and moving with the flow of energy instead of working against it.

Detachment

An important strength found in indigo is detachment. Manifesting includes envisioning results and then detaching from the outcome. Detachment is possible because you trust that what comes will be exactly what is best for you and others at this time, even when that involves the pain of lessons being learned. In relationships, it is equally important to detach from the outcome. When you suggest something to another person or you help that person through a difficult time in his or her life, you know that you cannot hang on to your perfect solution. Only that person can decide what to do. Only that person can take charge of his or her life.

Knowing When to Divulge Your Gifts

A strength found in indigo is to know what to share with whom. Not everyone is ready to hear what you know or to listen to what you have experienced. You know this and act accordingly. You respect the other person's boundaries; you understand that they will ask when they are ready to know more.

Lessons

Unbalanced indigo can become detached from the earth and day-to-day life. Within indigo are many gifts and abilities. In order to use these gifts in a balanced way, you need to stay close to your divine connection and to the earth. Accept your gifts with humility and grace.

Fear of What You Know

Because you seem to know things before they happen, you may fear this information. If an accident is about to happen or someone is going to die, this knowledge can be heavy and overwhelming. Indigo's lesson is to release responsibility for this information unless you are nudged by your inner wisdom to say or do some thing. You have the opportunity to bless those involved and ask that help be present for them. Your prayers can be of great assistance to them.

Expecting Others to Understand

Knowing what you know comes easily to you. If this knowing has always been part of your life, you may expect others to have received the same information or to be as intuitive as you are. Indigo's lesson is to accept others, whatever their abilities. What they know is what is right for them. Do not feel that you must share all that you know. Keep it to yourself unless you are guided to speak out.

Carrying Over Past Hurts

You may suspect or be aware of something traumatic that happened to you in another lifetime. You may be carrying hurt and pain from what another did to you in that lifetime. Often, you will recognize that person as someone who is in your life now. The lesson in indigo is to ask what you must do to clear this attachment to a past experience. Take responsibility for your part in the situation. Understand that both of you are meant to learn something from what you experienced. Imagine that you meet this person, discuss the situation, and clear it. This can all be done without involving the other person face to face.

Living Outside the Body

The difficulties of life on the earth may cause you to want to be absent. You may have known someone whose eyes indicated that his or her body was present, but inside, no one was home. Inner bliss can be so attractive that you lose your desire to be present in day-to-day life. Indigo's lesson is to live in the present on the earth. This is where you have come to finish your lessons, and this is where you have agreed to contribute what you can. You must bring yourself all the way into your body in order to be fully present. You must pay attention to the needs of your body in order to stay healthy.

Associating Only with Those Who Are Intuitive

Because your life seems so different, there may be a tendency to spend time only with others who understand your experiences. This limits your opportunities for growth. Indigo teaches you the importance of accepting all persons, no matter what their gifts and abilities. You may find that the person who sees only with physical eyes can teach you to see this world in a new way. The person who sees only through the eyes of a hurt inner child may teach you compassion and understanding for the human condition.

Grief

When the sinuses stuff up or a sinus headache comes on, you may be experiencing unshed tears of grief. Allowing yourself to know what has caused this pain will break the dam and release the tears. Breathing out the energy of grief as it is released will ease the pain. Indigo teaches you to pay attention to what you know, to accept what you know, and to offer compassion to the part of you that is in pain.

Not Being Taken Seriously

Because not everyone understands what you know, you may feel that you are being ignored or not being taken seriously. In fact, other persons may be afraid of what you know or afraid of what they do not understand. They may make fun of it or ignore it out of their own fear. Indigo teaches you to take your knowing seriously without expecting others to understand. Having others to talk to helps, but most of all, acceptance within you brings true inner peace.

Fear and Isolation

What you know and experience intuitively may set you apart. You may feel alone and isolated. You may experience depression or become wrapped in fear or immobilized by what you know and see. Accept your gifts for what they are. Find someone who has experienced all of what you are going through. This may be through a book you read or someone you meet. Have that person teach you how to deal with what you see through this different lense. These gifts are not abnormal; they are a heightened sense that has opened you to unfamiliar experiences.

Awakening

Indigo may be showing you that you are ready to awaken to a new level of awareness. This could be the time for you to open to your intuition and your other spiritual gifts. If you are ready, ask for these gifts to come; ask that those who are to help you discover these gifts will appear.

Responsibility

Intuitive gifts can be used to control others or bring you fame and fortune without regard for other persons involved. When you use these gifts in this way, they may hurt others. You are responsible for your gifts. Use them wisely. Never take others into fear or guilt. This will only block them and slow their progress. Allow your gifts to bring hope and healing to those who come to you.

Healing Exercise

If you tend to have headaches or tension at the base of your skull, this exercise may be for you. As you sit in quiet meditation, concentrate on a point in the middle of your forehead. This is the third eye. Visualize an eye that is lifting its lid, or see a flower opening petal by petal. You may need to unscrew a cap that is covering the opening. Allow whatever is inside this opening to come out. You may find that it has been blocked for some time. Move into the center of your head behind the third eye. This is the seat of the indigo color. Ask that this intuitive center be opened in its right timing at the right pace. Now, move to the base of the skull. On either side of the spine at the base of the skull, you may find tense muscles that cause headaches and pain. Keeping this indigo opening closed may be causing the pain. Find out what you are protecting. Ask yourself why you are afraid to open to your ancient knowledge and understanding. When you have assured your inner protection that it is safe to allow this part of you to open, you may find that the tension decreases and eventually disappears. Breathe through these openings and the middle of your head. Breathe in orange/yellow. Breathe out indigo. Do this often as you prepare to accept all that you know and all that you can know and experience.

Life Purpose

Healing

Your purpose may be to use your intuitive gifts to assist others. This could be as a medical intuitive, an intuitive assistant in an operating room or medical facility, as a spiritual intuitive, or simply as an intuitive friend. What you see or experience through your inner eye may bring understanding to the person you are helping. You may be able to pinpoint what is happening physically, emotionally, mentally, or spiritually. Often understanding precedes healing. You may be able to talk to parts of the body to help them heal. You may be able to connect the person to someone who has died in order to bring forgiveness and understanding to a relationship that was unfinished at the time of the death.

Using Ancient Knowledge

What comes through you from your past or future lives may be especially useful today. This knowledge may unveil new methods of healing people as well as the earth. It may enhance our understanding in many different areas of life.

Being a Conduit

Through your gifts, you may tap into information that comes from beyond you. This information may allow you to understand what is happening in the universe as well as on the earth. This conduit may bring music, art, science, philosophy, or another area of expertise to a new level of experience and understanding.

Teaching

You may be drawn to working with children who are already familiar with the gifts in the indigo color. These children are born knowing who they are. They are comfortable with their inner gifts. They will not tolerate untruth. These children may be misunderstood by others who consider their life-stance to be arrogant and stubborn. You may be able to help them accept and focus their gifts. You may also be drawn to teaching adults to open to their intuitive gifts or to accept what they are already experiencing. You may be led to help the public understand these intuitive gifts by teaching through books, films, poetry, art, or lectures.

Bringing in the Spiritual Blueprint

Open to the energy of indigo. Bring it in through the top of your head. Make your intent to be a conduit for ideas and understanding that are coming to you from your spiritual source. Sit with this energy. Hold a place for it in your heart center.

Lime Green

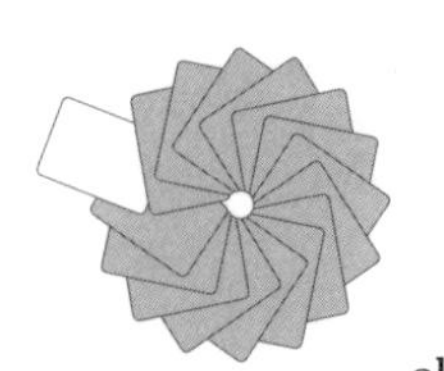

Lime Green is a powerful color. It is a combination of yellow and green. It brings together the empowerment and clarity of yellow with the love and understanding of green. Together this energy brings heart-centered power to a waiting world. Lime green is located at the tip of the breastbone between the heart and the solar plexus.

The color magenta balances Lime green. Breathe in magenta; breathe out lime green. These colors balance lime green's empowered heart energy with magenta's compassion for the whole world. Together they allow us to heal and transmute the energies that have taught us so much. Now we can open to a whole new way of living.

Strengths

Power

Your strength is the power you bring from deep within yourself. You operate with a self-assurance that sets you apart, yet you do not see yourself as above others. You are able to make clear decisions that take into account everyone and every aspect of the situation. You have no need to have power over others. Instead you seek to bring empowerment to all.

Fairness

Your greatest desire is to see everyone treated fairly. You encourage others to do their part, because you recognize the value of their contribution.

Natural Leadership

You do not consciously seek to lead; yet others recognize your natural leadership and automatically place you in that position. They recognize that you will be fair. They trust your honest and open way of relating to others. They do not fear your power and insight; they count on it. They see you as a balanced, caring leader.

Balance on All Levels.

Through the yellow in lime green, you are mentally sharp, always practical and clear. You understand human motivations. Through the green, you integrate all that you know with how you act. You open your heart without reservation, but never naively. You are dedicated to the good of all, yet you take care of yourself and do not give away your energy or power. You do what you love, not what you should do. Your friends and family never take a back seat. You spend time doing what you value.

Natural Boundaries

You have no trouble setting boundaries. Your clarity easily sees your limits, and your heart expresses those limits with love. You do not see boundaries as limiting or opposing others, but rather as a way of loving yourself and others.

Sharing

What you know is available to all. You have no need to keep what you know from others. You understand that we are all connected, that give-and-take creates a more complete whole.

Cooperative Clarity

You do not assume that you have all the answers. You encourage others to be clear and to share that clarity with the group. You know that each person's viewpoint is valuable.

Practical Caring

You value all aspects of life. Your caring extends to all. You do not expect something in return, nor do you expect others to respond in a certain way. Your caring is given without conditions. It is expressed in practical, down-to-earth ways. You are never above others. You are with them, but are not caught up in them.

Front-Runner

Your strength lies in your willingness to move out ahead of others. You are willing to investigate new ideas, new ways of doing things, while using your abilities to be practical and clear. You are not afraid of change, yet you embrace change only when it is in your best interest and seems to serve the whole.

Willingness to Help

You naturally step in wherever you feel you can help. This helping does not exclude others. You do not expect to be thanked for your help. It is as natural to you as breathing. Your help is never a burden or a power trip. It is what it appears to be.

Lessons

Lime green is such a powerful energy that when it is unbalanced, it can affect anything around it in a negative way. That is why it is so important to stay connected to the inner spiritual core when using this color. Only then can its great powers of healing and leadership be used to bring in a new age of love and understanding.

Coercive Power

When lime green is unbalanced, it leads to coercive power. You will tend to grab the power for yourself and expect others to appreciate your leadership even when it does not serve them. As you experience this power, your appetite for more power increases. You will draw in others for your own purposes. As others back away from your power in fear, you hold on more tightly. Your heart is closed. You have lost sight of the bigger picture. Lime green teaches you to come back to center. Know your own empowerment from within. Experience how much you are loved and valued. Learn to trust yourself and others. Trust that Divine Intelligence will work with you.

Negativity

Most of the lessons of lime green come from closing the heart and misusing power. You begin to see life as unfair. You are envious of those who seem to have more than you. You are critical of everyone around you, blaming them for anything that goes wrong or does not suit your preconceived ideas. Your expression and energy are harsh and acidic. Your ideas and suggestions are impractical. Lime green's lesson is to open your heart and claim your empowerment. Banish your fear through inner self-care. See your life from a balanced place within. Know that you are not alone. Feel the love that comes from your Source much like a Divine Parent.

Exclusivity

Unbalanced lime green closes you off from others. You turn inward. You look out for yourself and your family without regard to others. The lesson in lime green is to meet the fear that has closed you down. Bring it into your heart, into the wholeness of who you are. Then you will be able to open yourself again, and know the joy of sharing and cooperating with others.

Healing Exercise

Visualize yourself sitting in the garden in early spring before the flowers appear. Feel that energy moving up from the seeds. Feel the power of stems pushing out. Everything is fresh, alive and vibrant. Feel that same power within yourself. Notice how it comes from your center. It comes without pretense. It is natural, alive, and aware. Allow that power to move out into your limbs. Let it penetrate every cell in your body. Feel how alive and free you are. You feel good about yourself. Sit in this empowerment for as long as you wish. Consciously bring it into your everyday life.

Life Purpose

Leadership

You are a born leader. This comes to you naturally. Do not be surprised if you are called on to lead in many situations.

Cooperative Ventures

You will find yourself drawn to working with others to bring new ideas forward. Your practical, clear, heart-centered approach will be valuable in these ventures.

Setting Boundaries

You may be drawn into places where you work with others to set boundaries in a clear, loving way. Your approach will not wield familiar power, but your clarity and inner knowing can bring change just the same.

Balance

Your purpose may be to bring balance to any situation you encounter. Your ability to see all sides of a situation, your willingness to listen to other opinions while taking each person seriously, and your fairness and open-heartedness will be called upon.

Magenta

Magenta is a powerful color that is just now coming to our attention. Its ability to transmute unbalanced energy is more powerful than violet, and it carries within it a compassion more mature than what is offered through the color pink. It is located in a deep center of the heart although it is not traditionally associated with the heart chakra. It can also be experienced just above the top of the head. Magenta is made up of the passion and independence of red, the expansive possibilities in white, and the desire to speak out and change the world found in blue. Lime green is the color that balances magenta. From lime green comes openhearted, clear empowerment balanced by magenta's transforming compassion that is extended to the whole world.

Strengths

Powerful Transmutation

Magenta transmutes negative energy. It neutralizes the electrical charge that is created when energy is off balance. (Turn to the Healing Exercise for magenta to experience this transmuting power.) When magenta is your strength, you act as a transmuter of negative energy. You neutralize situations in which many emotions are running amuck. Others are drawn into the love you emit.

Compassion

Your compassion encompasses the whole world. It is your greatest desire for everyone to love life as much as you do. You wish to erase all the pain and suffering; yet, you know you are not to take away another's pain until that person is ready. Instead, you surround that person with your deep, unconditional love. Yours is an active compassion, so you do whatever serves the greatest good.

Spiritual Competence

You have matured in your spiritual life. Experiences that used to baffle or scare you no longer cause you concern. Your spiritual connection comes from the soul center, deep within your heart. From here, you are aware of yourself as a multidimensional being. You are operating on many levels besides this one. You are not attached to any particular form of spirituality, though you may still work within a religious structure. Your awareness allows that there are many paths to enlightenment. What each person understands through the soul center is his or her truth, and will lead that person to the path that was chosen for this lifetime. You have been willing to bring in all of your spiritual gifts. You have expanded into the height and breadth of who you are. You are comfortable as the expanded and competent person you are.

Dedication

Your dedication to wholeness is your strength. When others would give up on the world, you are steady on the course, knowing that all will come in its best timing. When others would condemn the world, you see the positive changes that give hope for the future. You work for wholeness in people, in communities, and the larger world.

Giving Something Back

From your positive and compassionate viewpoint, you feel blessed by all that you have experienced and those who have been in your life. There have been low points and high points, but all have brought you to this point. There has been pain and sorrow, joy and thanksgiving. All have contributed to the fabric of your life. None has been unimportant. You now feel ready to contribute from a place of gratitude, completion, and hope.

Passion

Though you are detached from specific outcomes in life, you are passionate about the process. There is nothing passive about you. Where there is injustice or corruption, you are willing to step in to see what can be done. Where there is suffering, you roll up your sleeves to find a way to help without making others dependent on you. Where there is misunderstanding, you ask for guidance for yourself and all others involved. Whenever possible, you bring a compassionate presence to the process.

Trust

Most of all, you trust yourself. You trust your inner guidance. You trust that you are supported from beyond yourself. All of this makes it possible for you to trust others. This is not a blind trust. This is a trust based on your understanding of human nature. You know that each person is operating as authentically as possible, given what he or she has agreed to work on in this lifetime. Trust includes knowing what to turn over to another and what to keep back, depending on what the person is able to handle. Clear communication replaces expectations. Compassion replaces caution. A belief that whatever transpires is working toward the greatest good for all replaces holding back. You are teaching the world a new way for people to relate to each other.

Bringing Change

For you, change is a natural part of life. As you and others see a need for change, you encourage people to work together toward that change. You assist, but do not insist. You encourage everyone to do what he or she feels led to do. As changes are made in communities, changes come to those working to bring in a new way of being together.

Celebration of Life

Whatever you are experiencing, even if it is difficult, you still touch into that place of deep joy. Gratitude is a way of life for you. You experience life fully through your senses, breathing in the fragrance of life in all its various forms. Moment to moment, you are present, and moment to moment, you stand in the presence of love. You live life fully from the center of your soul.

Lessons

The challenging side of magenta comes from an attachment to the world and a disconnection from the center of the soul. As magenta becomes balanced all its healing qualities become available.

Feeling Too Much

You tend to carry the ills of the world on your shoulders. It seems that no one is doing enough to end the suffering and humiliation that goes on every day. There is a compulsion within you to make the world change. It is time to step back to take a longer look. What are the lessons that are being learned through the suffering? For those who are making changes, what have they learned? What part of you is still suffering? As you complete your own inner healing, you will have more patience with those who are still in process.

Leaking Energy

There is a sense in which you may be bleeding from the heart. This is not a physical bleeding. This is an energy drain. If you extend your love to the whole world, but fail to keep an open flow of love coming in to you, you will feel drained. Compassion for the world is a wonderful gift that you give, but it must be accompanied by compassion toward the self as well.

Speaking Harshly

When you do not trust that there is a larger plan playing out in life, you may find yourself speaking out harshly against the ills of the world. This adversarial position creates negativity and self-protection in others, causing them to become entrenched in their own ideas and their own ways of doing things. Look inside to see what part of you feels alone and unprotected. What part of you needs to understand that you are part of a grand design?

Developing Safety

When distrust becomes pervasive, there is a tendency to build walls around yourself. These can be physical walls or energetic walls. What or who are you protecting yourself from? What has caused your mistrust? Repairing a sense of trust is an inside job. All the outer walls will not bring a sense of comfort and security. Finding the source of the mistrust, showing that part of you the truth, helping it to see that it is not alone, connecting it to divine guidance, and then taking baby steps toward trust will break the cycle.

Denying Spiritual Protection

When you are disconnected from the Source, divine protection seems like a hoax. Even when you push yourself to increase your trust, there may still be a part of you that is wary and continues to believe it is alone. What you envision, you will create. Take your distrust seriously. Some part of you has kept you from trusting because it has experienced the danger of trusting. Invite this part of you to meet your intuitive self. Bring this part of you into your heart to meet your competent self. Alone, you have no spiritual protection; connected to your center, you have all the help you will ever need.

Passion without Acceptance

You have a very passionate nature. You feel things deeply and you are drawn to act on what you feel. If there is still woundedness within you, there is a tendency to lash out at injustice and pain. This comes from an inner part of you that is still in pain. Your passionate, compassionate nature may then turn into attack and blame. Instead of an understanding heart, you extend non-acceptance. Do not in turn blame yourself for hardening your heart. Instead, take the steps to heal yourself. Then, you will be ready to help others without taking on their pain.

Taking Another's Lesson Personally

Feeling deeply is a gift and sometimes a trial. You feel others' pain and are deeply wounded by their anger. You may find that you blame yourself for their pain. Remember that their lessons belong to them. Become clear so that you can work with your own challenges while leaving the rest where they belong.

Healing Exercise

Imagine that there is an oval shape (like a tennis racket or dreamcatcher) that is sitting horizontally above your head high enough so that it sits outside your aura. There are strings of magenta that crisscross this oval. These magenta strands create an electrical field between them. Slowly bring this oval down through your aura and your body. If it stops, notice where it is in your body. This indicates a blockage. For example, if it stops at your throat chakra, you may need to speak up about something. As soon as you have discovered the source of this blockage, the oval will begin to move down again. When it reaches the ground, bring it into the earth. Then, start at the same place above your head again, bringing it slowly down through your aura and body. Do this a total of three times. By the last time, you will notice that the oval moves more easily and that you feel lighter. Thank magenta for its assistance in transmuting energies that you are finished with.

Life Purpose

Changing the World

In spectacular and unacknowledged ways you help to change the world. You are not content to experience the pain of the world without doing something to relieve that pain. Your magenta strengths give you all you need to help make those changes.

Healing

With magenta as your purpose, you will be shifting imbalance to balance, negativity to joy. These will be deep spiritual shifts that create pathways for others.

Showing the Way

Your spiritual maturity will show the way for others to follow. You will recognize the pitfalls for the compassionate. You will be able to help them crawl out of these places of anger and frustration to a place of balance, where they can truly make a difference.

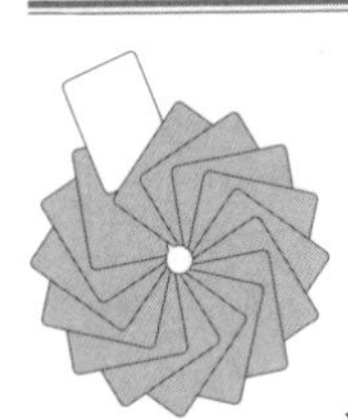

Orange

Orange combines the active, warm brightness of red with the fresh aliveness of yellow. This is the second chakra, which is located just below the navel. The balancing color for orange is blue. Breathe in blue; breathe out orange through this chakra for balance. Orange encourages you to feel feelings, and blue allows you to express what you feel.

Strengths

Feeling through All the Senses

You are alive and present. You experience life through the senses: touch, sight, sound, smell, and taste. The skin is an organ affected by orange, so touch is of great importance to you. Your world is full of music, art, fine food, and wonderful fragrances. These fine-tuned senses immerse you in what you love, lifting you into a lasting bliss.

Emotions

What you feel through the senses takes you deeper into the emotions. Smooth, loving voices register as an emotional response. A gentle, caressing touch communicates through the skin with deep emotional content. These emotions touch your heart. Your response is to love without restriction. You love your family, friends, partner or spouse, animals, and all living things. You love the rain, the sunshine, and wind at the beach. Whatever you feel touches you deeply.

Childlike Pleasure

Like a child, you explore the world through your senses. You don't hold back. Whatever catches your interest becomes your next avenue of exploration. Your fascination and complete appreciation of your world attracts and inspires others.

Vulnerability

Because you are so close to your emotions, you do not block what you feel. This includes difficult emotions as well as joy and laughter. Shutting off one emotion would mean shutting down the depth of your feelings. You honor all your feelings. If something hurts you, feeling that emotion is part of your healing.

Creativity

Your creative energy focuses through the senses. What you feel, you express. The materials you use creatively will often come from the earth or be made from earth's elements such as clay, stone, wood, glass, crystal, metal, seashells, flowers, and the like. You especially wish to mirror Earth's beauty and design.

Cheerfulness

You are naturally bright and cheery with a smile for everyone. Like a sunset, you exude warm comfort, with streaks of lightness and fun. Your laughter bubbles up freely and easily. You look for the best in everyone.

Affirming

Because you see the positive side of each person and circumstance, you mirror what you see. Others hear how beautiful or handsome they are, how able and intelligent, how comforting and loving. In your presence, they become what you see. They feel good about themselves.

Innocence

You tend to be fresh and innocent, wide-eyed with

surprise at a world that doesn't see through your eyes. How can they not see the beauty? How can they not see the wonder in each living thing? How can they miss the excitement of discovery in a world of such variety and complexity?

Integrity

You have nothing to hide. You tell the truth as you see it. You confess the slightest transgression because keeping it inside feels heavy, blotting out your brightness. You would not cheat at a game or tell an untruth about a friend. You are open, honest, and fair. You believe in the goodness of life.

Self-Respect

Even though you might desire something deeply, if it belongs to someone else you would not touch it or take it. You respect yourself, and you respect others. You would never knowingly hurt another person. You live your values openly and easily.

Sensuality and sexuality

Your body is your home. You are comfortable in your body. You like how it feels, how it can move you deep into the experience of the moment. Loving touch, perfume, music, and the taste of something sweet, such as chocolate, arouse your sensual nature. You are also comfortable with your sexual nature. For you, loving with your body is another way of loving with your heart and soul, a sacred experience that heightens and transcends the earthly sensual pleasures.

Lessons

Others can take advantage of the open innocence of orange. They can jealously tell you that you don't live in the real world. They can use you and manipulate your trusting nature. When that happens, orange becomes unbalanced through deep hurt.

Vulnerability

Because you feel so deeply, you may be vulnerable to overload. Anything that attacks the senses in an extreme way may cause you pain. Choose carefully what you expose yourself to—what movies or television you watch, the people you allow in your life, the foods you eat, and the music you listen to. All of these can wound you as well as move you.

Closing down

Your trusting, vulnerable nature can find the world a difficult place in which to live. Harsh words, rough touch, and foul smells can cause you to close down your senses. In the process, a piece of you dies. It is time to reclaim your sensual feeling nature; but this time, bring your capable, practical, aware self along with you. That way, you will be able to take care of yourself without having to shut down.

Weight Gain

You may have been vulnerable and trusting as a child, leaving yourself open to being sexually or emotionally abused. Not knowing how to protect yourself, you may have gained weight. The weight gain can seem like a protective barrier to that hurt child. In addition, you may have gained weight because you believe that if you are sexually unattractive, you will not have to face someone who might take advantage of you. Knowing this, you can make a decision to take this special child part of you into your heart. Help this child understand that you can now protect her or him. There is no longer a need to hide.

Addiction

When you have closed down to avoid hurt, you have opened yourself to addictions. These addictions are a way for the emotionally starved child within in you to seek satisfaction. You may eat to fill an emotional need. You may shop uncontrollably. You may watch TV incessantly. You may live through soap operas or romance novels, adventure novels, or murder mysteries to the place where your real life is on the back burner. You may work out or play sports to the exclusion of other parts of your life. You may seek out sexual liaisons to fill that empty place inside, even when you have a family you love and a partner you don't want to lose. You may take drugs to shut down the painful emotions that plague you. Drug addiction can include cigarettes, chewing tobacco, cigars, alcohol, over-the-counter medicine, caffeine in any form (chocolate, colas, coffee, tea), or illegal drugs. An addiction means that you consistently count on this substance to take away the pain or give you a feeling of well-being. Until you allow that child within you to feel again, by facing and healing the hurt, you will not be living fully.

Denying Creativity

You may have been forced to be perfect, or told so many times that you did things wrong, that you are afraid to tap into the creativity that is pushing its way to the surface. Will you do it right? Will others laugh at your creation or deny its worth? Who are you to think you have something to express or contribute? This part of you will only come forth when you embrace it. If you will assure your creative self that whatever it expresses will be accepted and appreciated by you, then it will feel confident enough to get started.

Hiding Your True Self

When you are vulnerable and have been hurt deeply,

you may hide your true self. Inside, you may feel dull and depressed, while outside, you smile and wear bright clothes. Inside, you may feel afraid and unsure, while outside you puff yourself up to look confident and assured. Inside, you may feel distrustful and angry, while outside you give without boundaries and manipulate others by making them dependent on you. You may be afraid of life, but you push yourself out into social situations, hoping to be accepted and liked. Again, the answer is to do what only you can do for yourself. Acknowledge who you truly are. Take satisfaction in who you are. Claim how special you are. There is no one else just like you. Decide to live from your authentic center, not to please anyone else, but to feel the satisfaction of being true to yourself.

Holding Back

If you have closed down your feelings, fear sets in. You may be afraid to spend money for fear there isn't enough. You may be afraid to give of yourself for fear others will take advantage of you. You may be afraid to express your love for fear it will be rejected or trampled on. Fear is only banished when you feel connected to the deepest part of yourself. Your divine center knows the truth. There is nothing to fear but fear itself. Even death is just a step into the next phase of life. As you become more authentic, you become more connected. As you become more connected, you know you are not alone. When you know you are not alone, you feel able to trust. When you trust, you are more able to let go of fear.

Sexual Guilt

If you grew up in a puritanical atmosphere, sensuality and sexuality may have been given a negative connotation. Your parents may have feared that you would tarnish your reputation or take advantage of another person.

Allow yourself to know that the body, with all its senses, is natural and good. How you react to your senses or feelings is a choice. How you treat others out of those feelings is a choice. If you honor your own body and your feelings, you will honor the body and feelings of the other person. If your senses become overwhelming and seem to be controlling you, pull them up into the heart center. Here, they are transformed. What you feel is energy. This energy can be used creatively; it can be used to express more love, and it can be used to enliven the inner life of the spirit. When appropriate, those sensual and sexual feelings can contribute to a deep and lasting, loving relationship.

Forgiveness

When you give yourself so completely, you can also be hurt deeply. Integrity is a cornerstone of who you are. You live in integrity yourself, and you expect others to do the same. When your trust is betrayed, the wound goes deep. You lose trust in others, but you also lose trust in yourself. How could you have missed the signs? How could you have overlooked the warnings? To heal this deep wound, you must remember that you are both here to learn. If we were perfect, there would be nothing to learn. Forgive yourself for being human. Forgive your betrayer for being imperfect.

Judgment of the Senses

If you were taught that sensuality and sexuality were "dirty" or "bad", you may find yourself judging others for their natural approach to their bodies. You may have that same voice inside, judging you for what you feel and what you want to experience. Ask your heart what is loving and true for you. Live your life from that truth and allow others to learn from their mistakes or live their own version of truth.

Judgment of Those Who are Closed

Because your body and its senses are a natural part of you, it may be difficult for you to accept and understand persons who are shut down and cold. If you will meet them in your imagination, you may encounter a frightened, hurting child inside of them trying to protect itself. Pray for that child. Ask that help will come to take that child out of its self-imposed prison. Open your heart to extend love, even if it is not reciprocated. Divine intervention has a way of surprising us with a change of our heart or a transformation of the most difficult person.

Healing Exercise

Eat an orange with all your senses intact. Smell its freshness. Feel the texture of its rind. Taste the sweet, tangy, meat of the orange. Allow the juice to dribble down your chin. Feel the satisfaction of having consumed something so alive and fresh. Enjoy the after-smell of orange on your fingers and face. Meditate with this smell. Imagine what it would be like if you were that fresh, alive, tangy, sweet, textured, and juicy. Let this image penetrate to your core. If you wish, choose to become what you imagined. Allow it to be as real in your outer world as you felt it in your inner world. Thank the orange for what it has taught you.

Life Purpose

Motivator

You may be drawn to become an Actor, Comedian, Coach, Salesperson, Counselor, or Parent. Understanding emotions and what drives people from within will certainly mold your life purpose. You can use this understanding to help others live from the best that is in them.

Life Cheerleader

A cheerleader in life affirms others in the best way possible. You become someone who believes in them when they may not yet believe in themselves. You can encourage them to trust themselves and find their empowerment from within.

Sunshine

Your purpose may be to bring a brightness to life. Those who have lost hope or are mired in depression may be helped by looking up and seeing that there is joy and happiness available after all. Those who grew up in a cold, rejecting environment can experience warmth and affirmation. Being who you are is enough. The rest will take care of itself.

Creativity

Through your creativity, you can bring joy and appreciation for beauty to yourself and others. This can be as simple as arranging flowers in a vase or carving a figure out of wood, or as big as creating a blueprint for a special building or building a structure from the ground up.

Working with Addicts

You may have experienced addiction yourself, so you know the trap that is there when emotions are closed down. From what you have learned, you may be able to help others turn their lives around.

Respect for the Body

You may be drawn to become a Body builder, Athlete, Health and Fitness Teacher, Model, Health Counselor, Weight Reduction Therapist, Physical Therapist, Dentist, or Health Practitioner. All of these professions come from those who pay attention to the body. Each requires proper nutrition, exercise, and special treatment of the body. Your life purpose may be to help yourself and others treat the body with respect and the care that makes it possible to enjoy life through the senses. Pain, fatigue, weight concerns, or any other bodily ailments or aberrations stand in the way of healthy sensuality.

Pink

Pink combines the vitality of red with the purity of white. Since pink is so light in color, the purity and floating nature of pink predominate. The balancing color for pink is light green. This is the green of the heart mixed with white. Pink is the softness and floating purity of love, while light green is the soft, earthly grounding of love. Through the heart, breathe in light green; breathe out pink.

The lessons available through pink go through a tempering process. As if through a chemical change, pink transmutes to silver. The pain of betrayal turns into a deep understanding of how take care of yourself without closing off from others. Hurt feelings are healed leaving a deep understanding of those who are wounded.

Strengths

Innocence

In your innocence, you don't pay attention to the harsh realities of the world. You don't allow them to touch your bliss. You see everything in its purity and love. You travel through life as if in a pink bubble.

Childlike

Life is a playground. There is so much to enjoy! There are no cares, no worries, nor any dangers. Everything is perfect. Everything is available for your enjoyment. You dance with the fairies and swing on a star. Everything is possible. What others consider unreal seems perfectly natural to you.

Playfulness

You wish everyone would see the fun in life the way you do. You want everyone to join in.

Freedom

You feel free to explore and experience without restriction. Responsibilities do not weigh on your shoulders. They belong to someone else. Your job is to show others how to have fun.

Trust

You trust others completely. You expect them to be as innocent and pure as you are. You trust in the good in all things.

Generosity

You give of yourself without restriction. You give whatever you have to whoever needs it. You believe there is more where that came from.

Love

You love without restriction. Your love encompasses all people, animals, flowers, plants, and all other living things. You love their strength and beauty and their abilities and gifts. You are never jealous of the beauty in others, because you accept the beauty in yourself as well. You love yourself without restrictions. You see no flaws in yourself or others.

Kindness

If you see tears in someone's eyes, you stop to help them brush them away. You sit near them just to let them know they are not alone. You take flowers to neighbors and friends just because. You stop to visit someone who is sick. You send cards for every occasion.

Hopefulness

Even when things around you are less than perfect, you live in hope that they will soon be better. You do not blame others or yourself. You accept what is and go on with hope in your heart.

Imagination

Because you do not restrict yourself to only the mundane, you can create a whole world through your imagination. The restrictions found in what others see are left behind. Yours is a colorful palette. Possibilities are endless.

Strength

The strength in pink is subtle. At first, others may see you as soft, not strong. Yet, your strength is in your loving nature. Because you are not a threat, others let the barriers down. You seem to walk in where no one else could. When the walls are down, the healing may begin.

Safety

Others feel safe with you. Children are drawn to you. They know that you will accept them and hold them. They love your playfulness. The world seems right and good when you are around.

Lessons

The challenging side of pink is its vulnerability without protection. When this vulnerability is compromised, great hurt results. The lesson in pink is to never lose that childlike joy and innocence while allowing the capable part of the self to protect you and help you live in a world that does not always respect innocence.

Unrealistic

Because you live in a land of trust, hope, and imagination, you often do not see what is happening around you. Others may be taking advantage of you. Your life may not be as idealic as you thought. When you realize what is happening, you may go into hiding or depression. The lesson in pink is to see and accept what is human, but to never lose your childlike innocence. Do not go into situations without seeing them for what they are, but still find that beauty that is also present.

Dependency and Innocence

Since you tend to be unfamiliar with the world as others experience it, you may become dependent on others for practical, everyday needs. This dependency can leave you vulnerable to those who would take advantage of you. If someone handles your money, that person may be siphoning off some for himself or herself. You are likely paying too much for services because you are unaware of the going rate. The lesson in pink is to pay closer attention to what is happening around you without becoming suspicious and wary. Ask questions even when others become uncomfortable with the questions. Focus some of your attention on your day-to-day life so that you can be present and aware.

Avoiding Responsibility

Responsibility may seem heavy and unrewarding. You may go on ahead with your life without noticing that you didn't do what you said you were going to do; or you didn't communicate with others, so they were left waiting for an answer. You don't mean to be unkind or put someone else out. You just don't want to be restricted. The lesson in pink is to be aware of others without making that awareness become a burden. Don't promise something unless you are sure you can follow through. Do your part so that others are not left with all the work.

Let others know what they need to know so that they can also get on with their plans.

Avoiding Unpleasantness

" If you don't pay attention to it, it will go away." That kind of thinking often gets you into trouble. What is unpleasant often does not go away. It comes back later, only then it is more sticky and messy than when it first came to your attention. The lesson in pink is to pay attention. See what is there. Deal with it now so that you are done with it. Then you can get on to more pleasant things.

Avoiding Anger

You are very uncomfortable with anger, whether it's yours or someone else's. You will walk on eggshells to avoid making someone else angry. You will talk yourself out of how you feel in order to avoid your own anger. You will take the blame even when you are not at fault just to shift the energy, because anger makes you so uncomfortable. The lesson in pink is to notice anger, decide if you are to do something about it, and then act. Sometimes this will require you to set boundaries. This is not easy for you, but is very important in order to stay balanced. You may need to insist that the person who is angry take a time-out and then come back to clear up what is bothering her or him. Your own anger is a signal to pay attention. Something has triggered a sensitive place within you. Likely, there is healing needed there.

Unrequited Love

Because you love so easily and completely, you may be surprised and deeply hurt when that love is not returned. What you thought was love from another person may have been manipulation. Your innocence and straightforward openness can set you up to be used. Since you see only the fine parts of the other person, manipulation and hidden agendas don't even occur to you. You feel blindsided. You didn't see the blow coming. The lesson in pink is to look deeper. Is what you see true? Are you looking past something that is right in front of you? Are you overlooking traits that indicate hidden agendas? Don't shut down your way of loving. Do be more discriminating in how you pour it out. Be sure you see what is truly there.

Need for Love and Attention

You like to be the star. You like to have everything revolve around you. You are kind and loving, but on your terms. You want your needs filled immediately. The lesson in pink is to give yourself the attention you need by turning that kindness and love to the part of you that is seeking to be noticed. Fill your own inner needs so that you may then turn your attention outward, without looking to others to fill you up. You will then be more aware of the needs of others and be able to take them into account.

Hopelessness

Your bubble can burst at some time in your life. What you thought was true now seems to be a lie. Your future seemed to be full of wonderful things to come, but all of that may now seem unreal. The lesson in pink is to keep hope alive, but know that others do not always live the truth. Surround yourself with those of integrity. Realize that being human means learning lessons. If you miscalculated a person or event, know that you can learn from it. You don't need to experience that again as long as you have finished the lesson.

Overburdened

Your sensitive nature can be quickly weighted down. Remember that your playfulness, inventiveness, and freedom to be are like the breath of life. Without them, life becomes stale and out of balance. Take time to be, to play, and to enjoy the day.

Healing Exercise

Find a quiet spot to sit and relax. Use your imagination to see yourself floating on a pink cloud. Feel how safe and comfortable you are. There is a rocking motion that is soothing and comforting. Stay with this feeling for a while. Now rouse yourself a bit. Peek over the edge of the cloud. Look down at your life as it is. What do you see? Do you like what you see? From this perspective, what might you change? What would you do more of? When this feels finished, have your cloud gently drop you back to Earth. Come into the present moment. Write down what you saw and what you want to change. Consider the best way to begin.

Life Purpose

Bringing Simple Joy

Your fresh, simple approach to happiness and joy will remind others to let go of the complicated lives they are living. They will be brought back to playfulness and openhearted loving.

Bringing Hope

In a world that reads of tragedy daily, there is a tendency to see only what is wrong. You remind others to look for all the good in people and situations. You bring hope to a weary world.

Advocacy for the Children

Your childlike nature looks out for children. You want to give them safety and nurturing. You want them to be free to laugh and enjoy life. You want them to know they can be who they are because they are beautiful just as they are.

Laughter

You laugh at yourself. You laugh at life. Your laughter is infectious. It never embarrasses others, nor does it take advantage of another's weakness. You laugh with the world and yourself, not at the world.

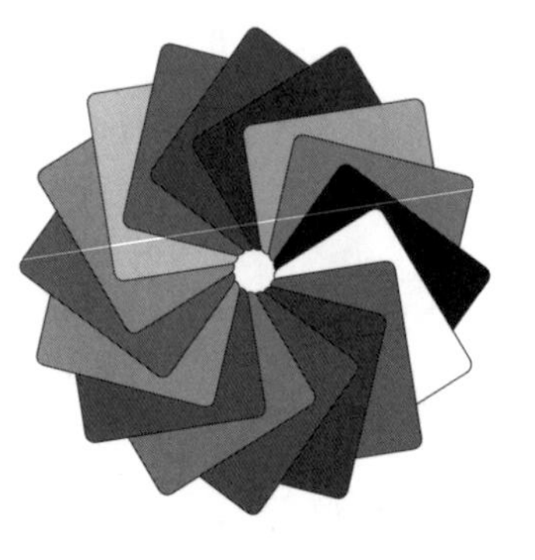

Red

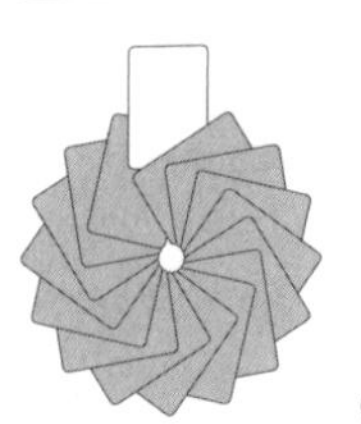

Red gains its strength from the molten core of the earth. It creates a stable foundation for the whole energy system of the body. Red is the first chakra energy center. It is located at the base of the spine. The balancing color is green. Red explodes with energy that green channels into creation.

Strengths

Initiating

You are full of energy. Your energy fires up the creative force that starts projects. Once the project is well underway, you are bored. It's time to start something new. Be sure to set up your projects so that others are ready to pick up where you left off. Let others know that you will be doing only the beginning work.

Passion

Whatever you take on, you are passionate about. You will explain it and defend it until others agree.

Versatility

Sometimes your passion spills over into more than one project at a time. You can handle it. Your skills are many, and you juggle your many activities adeptly. You are confident that you can take on most anything that is set before you.

Independence

You would rather develop your own business than work for someone else. You enjoy working with others, but you have no patience for the hoops you must jump through for a large organization. Sometimes you push on ahead even if someone else could do the work, because your timetable is "now" and his or her timetable is "later." You appreciate others' ideas, but you prefer to have the final say. That way, you know it will be done the way you want.

Foundation

You are a foundation builder. You see the big picture. From it, you know what has to be in place first. That's your job. Once the building blocks are in place, you give the job to someone else.

Courage

When others hesitate, you move forward. Often you find that you are plowing new ground and creating new pathways ahead of everyone else. When others say it can't be done, you find a way. When others say there's no time, you make time. Your passionate nature forges ahead against all odds.

Survival

Your physical survival is never in question, because you know that you will do whatever it takes to survive. Your force of will, alone, can move mountains. To you, there are always options. Even what seems like an obstacle to others seems like an opportunity to you.

Sexuality

Your sexual nature is red hot. You are passionate, involved, and eager.

Involving others

Even though you prefer to work on your own, you like to involve and encourage others. You work especially well with those who have a similar fast pace.

Spontaneity

You like to act on your spontaneous ideas. You seem to feel immediately whether the idea will work or not. Others are swept up in the movement you create, even if they would rather plan ahead.

Manifesting

You can bring into form most anything you envision. You feel its completed blueprint even before you start. Your passion fuels this creative process. Once you are in motion, others stand back waiting for your instructions.

Seductiveness

Your primal energy is seductive. Others are taken in easily. They feel alive and energized when they are around you. Juices are flowing. Excitement is high. There is no doubt that they will have a good time in the flow of your energy.

Lessons

When the first chakra energy center is blocked, the passion, fire, and drive have to go somewhere. This can lead to anger, sore joints, exhaustion, and bullheadedness. Open this energy center and you will have all your energy back so that you can use it to live to its fullest.

Burnout

The danger is that you will spew out so much energy that there will not be time to replace it. Burnout results. This leaves a project half finished, with others standing around wondering what to do. Your body feels used up. Your lesson is to recognize this tendency, slow down a bit without losing your enthusiasm, and take the steps one at a time.

Few Boundaries

Your movement is so fast-paced that you spend little time considering what you are doing. You tend to give out all you have. Others will gladly use your energy as long as you give it up. At some point, you will discover that you gave more than you intended. Anger may set in. You may blame the person you gave your time and energy to. The lesson is to set your boundaries. Know what you will and won't do. Feel when you are overextended so that you can pull back. Refuse to blame yourself or someone else. Instead, learn from what you have experienced.

Pushiness

Unbalanced red energy sees only the goal or need to finish the project. There is no room for excuses or lateness. You tend to push others as hard as you push yourself. This creates resentment. No one wants to work with you. The answer is to pace yourself. Make sure your life is balanced in all areas. Trust that the timing will be perfect. Take pleasure in each step along the way.

Loss of Interest

Since you like the excitement of starting the project, finishing it seems less glamorous. The work becomes tedious, not fun. The lesson is to know your abilities. Sign up for the part you enjoy. Be the starter energy, and leave the rest to someone else. There are those who would rather work with a project once it is under way. Avoid feeling guilty about not finishing the project. Be sure you have been clear with everyone involved that you will step away as soon as the project is under way.

Incompletion

You are great at getting things going, but often leave projects unfinished. This may be an opportunity to learn discipline. Look at what needs to be done. See how you can make the process fun for you. Invite others to join you.

Not Listening

Because your mind is working so fast, you may not hear what someone else is saying. You have formulated the answer even before that person has finished speaking. You devalue others when you do this. This can also lead to an unwillingness to take advice. You have to try it out for yourself. Consider how much energy you waste this way. Relax, stop what you are doing, and focus your attention on the one who is speaking. Hear every detail before you consider answering. Mull over what has been said before you make a decision. Others will value the way you take them seriously.

Anger and Frustration

Unbalanced red doesn't like to be slowed down or hemmed in. You want to be free to move at a fast pace and work as long and hard as you want. When others suggest a more balanced approach, you are likely to flare up. If others don't work as fast or hard as you do, you become frustrated and judgmental. Now is the time to accept that everyone has his or her own pace. By asking the person how soon something can be ready, you can stop looking for it sooner. By allowing yourself some slack, you can move into a more balanced flow. When anger and frustration continue to leak out from the first chakra, the red energy can end up in the joints of the body, causing inflammation, swelling, and pain. When the part of you that feels frustrated is allowed to vent and then given the opportunity to flow through the heart, you may find the pain diminishing.

Survival

A closed first chakra causes fear. There is distrust so great that you think you will not survive. You worry about money, control, job security, safety of your family, and more. You lose your ability to manifest anything, and your drive and vitality disappear. Often, holding on tighter increases the fear. Trust may be the answer. Trust comes when you feel well cared for. This is a difficult lesson, because it requires you to reestablish your relationship with the earth and with your divine center. Once that connection is made, the fear will dissipate. Detaching from the outcome will also lessen the fear. Turn to the section on brown to connect to the earth. Turn to the section on green and violet to connect to the divine.

Seductiveness

This can be a positive trait, but it can also contain a lesson. When seduction is used to entrap other persons or manipulate them, it has lost its balance. This takes away the other person's choice. Notice your motivation. Are you relaxed and free, or are you calculating and tight? Let go of your need to control. Reclaim the excitement and passion of the moment. Disconnect from your need for others to join in.

Consuming

When the first chakra is closed down, you feel a lack of energy. You may try to find that energy in someone else. Others may feel that you are draining them. They will want to avoid you. When your focus is so tight that you see only your own needs, others may find they have been pulled into your limiting circle as well. This tends to encourage others to let go of responsibility for their own ideas and direction and will tend to pull them away from their own life path. They may feel you are all consuming. You take them in and burn them out. Step back. Discover why you are closed to the red energy. Listen to your heart for the answers. Allow your focus to clarify your next step, but do not allow your focus to keep you from seeing the complete picture.

Spell-Binding

Red gives you charisma. When this charisma is used to further your own ends, or if it is used to convince others that you have all the answers, you are misusing the power found in red. Those who are vulnerable may follow you without listening to their own inner wisdom. They may act as if they are under your spell. Break the spell. Discover why you need others to place you above them. Use your powers and ability to encourage others to grow and gain confidence in themselves. Encourage them to trust their own inner knowing. Connect to your divine center so that your power may be used for the greatest good for yourself and all others.

Healing Exercise

As you sit in quietness, picture the molten core of the earth as if it were the center of a volcano. Feel its vitality and strength. Allow this energy to move up through the earth, into the bottoms of your feet, up your legs, and into the base of your spine. This is the center of the red energy. Breathe into the red energy. Feel how you are connected to the earth. Experience your vitality increasing, your focus clearing. Breathe green into the heart. Then, breathe out red. Do this four more times. Feel the balance develop. Sit in this balance for as long as you wish.

Life Purpose

Business Owner

You are well suited to run a business. Your independence, ability to get things moving, and your willingness to include others will all serve you well.

Motivator

The fire and passion that you bring to life will inspire and motivate others. You can then help them find their own inner fire.

Salesperson

You have the kind of energy that reaches out to people. Your ready smile and enthusiasm will encourage customers to come to you.

Group Leader

Your leadership centers in your ability to bring others on board in a cooperative effort. Your energy will spark others to become enthusiastic about their work.

Silver

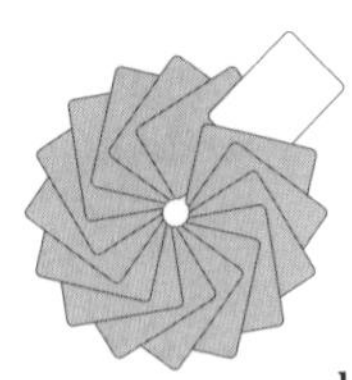

From all that you have learned in your life and perhaps, in many lifetimes, you have gained great wisdom. You have learned to stay bright even in the most difficult circumstances. You have been tempered by your experiences. What is left is shining sliver. Silver does not come from a chakra center in the body. Instead, it can be used with other colors, or it can stand on its own. Silver and gold bring high vibrations of female and male energy. Even though these colors are not breathed into the body for balance, they still bring balance to the dualities of female and male energies in this world.

Strengths

Shining in the Darkness

Like silver, you have been tempered by your experiences. What were once lessons in the midst of transformation (represented by black) now shine brightly. Darkness cannot hide or shut out the brightness that is within you. You stand as an example for others who are moving through their lessons. Like a silver ray of moonlight on a dark night, you bring light into the midst of negativity, grief, suffering, and hopelessness. Others feel that they can persevere because they see that you have come through extreme circumstances with an inner shine of love and caring. When others look into your eyes, they know the pain that you have suffered, but they also see a bright, deep light and a compassion born of that suffering.

Flowing

You carry yourself with a flowing confidence. Whether you are a man or a woman, your inner feminine energy creates beauty for you and for others. You comfortably move through your day, touching others with your grace. You gently encourage and affirm those around you. You are highly valued by all.

Valuing the Past

The past is important to you. It has transformed you into what you are today. This may include experiences in this lifetime and in past lifetimes. As you look to the silver moon, you feel the presence of all that is past. In gratitude, you sit in quiet respect.

Wisdom

When lessons are finished, they are replaced by wisdom. The wisdom within you shines through your eyes. Nothing can take that away from you. You are so very present, yet you seem lovingly detached. There's nothing that can push you to go faster than the pace of your own flow. Nothing will surprise you. You have seen it all. You smile, knowing there is a lesson in process.

Celebration

Each moment is precious. You linger a moment longer to feel deeply. Each person is precious. You caress others with the tenderness that shines from your eyes. The silver that adorns your body and your home symbolizes what you value and celebrates the past, present, and future. It is brought out on special occasions. Its festive shine lights up your home and welcomes family and friends alike. Memories are shared. New lives are honored. Time stands still to mark of what is shared.

Cherishing

You cherish all that graces your life, the joy and sorrow alike. You have come to accept the ebb and flow of the human experience. You have come to know that pain teaches the deepest lessons. You know the courage it takes to face those lessons. You accept and cherish each person whether he or she chooses to accept the lesson or leaves it to another time and space.

Intent

You have come to respect the power of intent. You choose wisely that which you envision, knowing that your every thought connects to the source of creation. Your desire quickly becomes your reality.

Holding the Light

You hold the light on a clear path for those who follow you. Where you have been in your experiences now clears the way for others. What took you many years to discover and understand can now be learned at lightning speed. Transformation shifts reality in the blink of an eye.

Alchemy

You have the ability to turn what is dark into the brightness of silver. What you have learned through your experiences, and what you know within you gives you the ability to transmute unbalanced energy into balanced, shining light. Continue to use this ability to help yourself and others.

Lessons

Lessons from silver come to those who have not embraced the learning that has presented itself. This tarnishes the silver. Its beauty is hidden and the darkness still remains. It is time to allow the light to shine through the darkness, to let the beauty of silver shine through.

Denying the Past

Your past experiences are calling to you to embrace them. You have been denying what was done to you and denying what you have done. Lying only increases the pain. Come clean. Know that what has been done can teach you powerfully. As you tell the truth to yourself and others, the healing may begin.

Bemoaning the Past

You cry out against what you have experienced. "It isn't fair!" you say. "Why me?" "Why have others avoided this kind of pain?" These are important questions. The answers will lead you to peace inside. Remember that this life is like a drama unfolding on a stage. You are the playwright, the set designer, and the director. However, once the play begins, the actors are on their own. The drama you have written is there for your greater benefit. If you will find the gift within the pain, you will move into the peace of knowing that you learned what you had set up for yourself.

Putting Beauty Away

When life seems hard and unyielding, it is difficult to appreciate the beauty around you. But, doesn't that just increase the pain? Turn again to find the beauty in the midst of the unbeautiful. Pay attention to simple beauty: acts of kindness, the gift of a smile, sunshine after the rain. This is the beginning of wisdom. Like the other side of a coin, beauty is closer than you think.

Straightforwardness

You are tired of deception and untruths. People need to face the truth! You tell them the truth whether they want to hear it or not. But, what is the truth? Is what you see in others inside of you? Are you living in deception and untruth? See the mirror that others hold for you. Accept what lies within you. When you do this, amazing changes in your perception will occur. You will either see others in a new light, or they will have disappeared from your life. Poof! You changed the scene.

Anger at Yourself

How could you have become caught in such a tangled web? How could you have sold out on yourself—compromised your integrity? For what? Can you forgive yourself? Can you accept that what you did is part of your learning? Accept that you are human. Send blessings to those who may have been hurt by you. Begin again as a changed person.

Shutting Down

Pain and suffering have taken their toll. You have decided that there is no integrity in the world. You have to look out for yourself since no one else will. You have become cold and calculating in your relationships. You refuse to share what you have learned with others. Your loving nature has turned cold and hard as metal. You have now become the perpetrator as well as the victim. Choose now to break the cycle. Polish away the tarnish. Let your light and love shine out. Feel fresh and alive again.

Obsession with Ritual

"Perhaps if I repeat the ritual from the past, it will magically transform my life; that way I won't have to face this pain." "If I just bring the family together one more time, maybe the love and caring will be there." "If I use Mom's favorite recipe, her love will be in our midst." It is not the ritual that makes things right. Ritual can help to bring healing, but only if you are willing to heal or you are ready to turn and move through the lesson. Ask for help. Open your heart. Surrender to your inner wisdom and power.

Negativity

You have lost hope and trust in life. It seems that there is only pain and suffering. You have succumbed to telling half-truths to increase your advantage. You gossip about those who seem to have it better than you, or you put down others to make yourself feel better. You brood over lost dreams and an uncertain future. You live from a pretense so as to avoid exposure of what goes on beneath the surface. What you put out comes back to you. The people who are drawn to you are morose and negative as well. They bemoan the state of the world. Isn't it time to lift this cloud of grief and self-pity? See what you can gain from what has come across your path. Use your intent to chart a new path. Seek out others who are finding their way out of the pit of negativity. Ask your guardian angel to enfold you in its wings to give you the strength and comfort to change your direction.

Attracting Life Drama.

You may find that you are attracting persons who are in the midst of very difficult life experiences. There is a danger that you will be pulled into their emotional distress. Drama can seem exciting because it stimulates the adrenaline. Soon, you may find yourself increasing the drama by repeating all that is happening or by involving others. Step out of the drama. Gain perspective by becoming the observer. What do you see? Is this what you want to experience? By stepping back, you can disengage from the drama. Now you may help yourself and be available to help the other persons involved.

Healing Exercise

What would it be like if this were your last day on Earth? What would you notice? Would you spend your time on gossip or self-pity? Or would you look around you to see a smile here, a touch of kindness there? Notice that older couple across the way exchanging a look of tenderness and love. Watch the kitten chase its tail. Thank the birds for their songs. Feel your breath as it moves in and out. Divine love flows in with every breath. How can you simplify your life? How can you put your attention to what really matters? What do you need to do to shift your perspective? Write in your journal about how you feel, who you want to be, who you are inside, how you can begin again. Congratulate yourself for having the courage to say "yes" to change.

Life Purpose

Bringing Wisdom

What you have experienced can free others to live from their best self. Your wisdom needs to be shared. Begin in simple ways. Your children, grandchildren, or other children in your life can benefit from a word here, a pat on the back, a knowing smile. Search your heart for how you are to share what you have learned.

Carrying the Light

When you were at your lowest, was there someone there for you? Did someone hold a ray of light for you? If not, you know what would have helped. If they did, you know how much that helped you. Now is the time for you to do that for someone else. Seeing divine light fall around another person blesses them in ways you may never really know.

Opening the Way

Someone has to be willing to be the lead goose. Someone has to fly at the front of the wedge. Is that you? What you have come through may have straightened the path for someone else. Is there more that requires your strength and courage?

Offering Ritual.

Your role is to remember ritual, to offer others the opportunity to mark special times in special ways, to light a candle for the one in need. Others may not know the value of ritual. You can show them how to bring closure to a death, celebrate a birth, and bring Presence to a transition. How you do this will be unique. Feel it, allow it, and appreciate the opportunity to help.

Healing the Feminine Energy

If yours has been a path to reclaim your inner feminine energy, you may be ready to offer that learning to others. Or, perhaps you are simply to transform that energy by living out of your true inner female, by celebrating the feminine energy within you. Consider that holding and expressing the true female brings change as you join others in the same process.

Turquoise

Turquoise is blue with some green added. It is not a traditional chakra energy center, but does work like a chakra. It is located between the throat chakra and the heart chakra at the position of the thymus gland. Just as the thymus gland functions to ward off imbalance in the body through the immune system, the turquoise energy center keeps us balanced by keeping our life purpose on track. The blue in turquoise assists in the expression of the life purpose, and the green integrates that purpose into both the human and divine aspects of life. It is from the heart that we know our life purpose. It is from the turquoise that we say “yes” to what we agreed to in this life.

Strengths

Owning Up to Your Life Purpose

You may not fully understand your life purpose, but you have said “yes” to it. This means that you are willing to follow your inner guidance wherever it takes you. You trust the plan. You have agreed to be part of this plan. You are willing to go through the preparation that your lessons are bringing you. You know that those you love may not understand, at least not for now. This makes the process harder, but to back out now would be like dying inside. You are ready to move forward.

Self-responsibility

You know that what happens in your life is up to you. As much as you might like someone else to take over at times, you know that you will not allow that. You value the input from trusted friends, but decisions you make about your life are yours. Consequences from those decisions are yours as well. You don't expect others to bail you out if life gets tough. Advice from others is heard and accepted, but not always followed. You keep your larger mission in life in focus at all times. What may seem logical to others may not suit what your life is really about. Only you can make that final determination. You allow others that same responsibility. You do not try to step in or change their minds. You affirm their desire to make their own decisions.

Accepting the Expansiveness of Your Life Plan

Your life plan may be so all-encompassing that you see only a small portion of where it will take you. This doesn't necessarily mean that your life will be in lights. The immensity of how we can affect others, our world, and ourselves through our actions on the inner realms is beyond our human comprehension. Our beingness expands far beyond our body, affecting whatever it touches. Our thoughts create and discreate from day to day. When these powers are used consciously, there are no limits. You are willing to be that expansive, that powerful, and that effective.

Humanitarianism

While each of us has a soul purpose, we are also all connected. The Source from which everything emanates is energy. We are offspring of that Source. In a family, parents are always connected to the children in some way, and the children are always connected to each other. It is the same with a spiritual family. We are all connected through the heart. It is natural, then, that we help each other. What happens to one person affects us all. This connection can never be broken. You have chosen to consciously act from that connection. You expect synchronicity in your life that comes from this connection. You have made yourself available to assist your brothers and sisters and all created forms in whatever way possible.

Salt of the Earth

You are what we all strive to be, balanced in body, mind, and spirit. This did not come easily to you, yet you now wear it with ease. You are relaxed and comfortable with yourself. You trust yourself, your intuition, and your abilities. You value your mind and your body. You treat them with respect, while allowing that deeper part of yourself to lead the way. Others feel comfortable in your presence. Just as salt brings out the flavor of food, you bring out the essence of life.

Following the Heart

What you sense and feel through your heart, you allow in your life. You trust what comes from the soul center of your heart. This is your connection to the Source. This is your connection to the earth. From here, you integrate your life. What your life is about fuels your thoughts, actions, and responses. What you value engages your time and energy. All works together for fulfillment and the joy of living.

Allowing

You allow your life to unfold naturally. Where others may force an outcome, you quietly wait, knowing you will be shown the next step. This flow allows for synchronicity of events. Someone will cross your path when he or she is needed. An idea will surface that coincides with other events. A book will be given to you that answers the question you have barely formulated. This allows life to come to you. There is peace in this way of living. You trust life's flow. You leave the outcome to that part of you that sees a bigger picture.

Peace

Your heart desires peace in the world. You know that this will only come as each person and each nation finds its way to wholeness. You are open to participating in this process of peacemaking. You know that your part begins by finding your own inner peace and living from the heart in all of your relationships. Setting boundaries from the heart creates clarity and respect. Listening to others from the heart allows you to see from another's point of view. All of this is part of peace as well.

Lessons

The lesson in turquoise is to stop avoiding or denying your life purpose. This can lead to depression. At one's lowest ebb, life itself may seem without meaning. Hiding out from what your life is about often comes from fear. As you face this fear, you are able to claim a deeper meaning in life and are willing step out in faith to do what you came to do.

Avoiding your Life Purpose

You have moved your life purpose to the back burner. You may be denying that it exists at all. Confusion and self-doubt are great ways to set up a smoke screen that says you don't know what your life is really about. Does life seem dull and drab? Do you seem to be sad and depressed? We came here to learn something and to give something back. When we don't do that, everything seems off. Nothing seems to satisfy. Find a way to get to the bottom of your reluctance. Seek out others who are resonating to their life purpose. Support yourself emotionally as you step forward onto your unique path.

Denying Responsibility

Are you making others responsible for your life? This can mean other people or institutions. You can allow teachers, parents, a spouse, the church, school, or anyone else to be responsible for your beliefs and actions. If something goes wrong, there is someone or some place to blame. It is time to drop that pretense. You have always been responsible for your life, because it is your life. Allowing a void to develop because you have failed to exercise that responsibility can lead to sidetracks in life. This is not necessarily a waste. On those side roads, you can discover and learn much that will be useful when you finally resume your journey.

Feeling Discounted

You have a great need for others to take you seriously. You constantly work to prove to others how much you know and how much others value what you know. This doesn't fill the void. You still feel slighted and discounted. It is time to value yourself from the inside out. What you value, others will value. Only you can fill that need inside to be counted as special.

Controlling your Life

When you have lost trust in your life direction, the human part of you attempts to control what comes into your life and what you give out. You become convinced that others want to take something away from you, so you stay alert to how others might take advantage of you. Because you feel isolated and alone in figuring out your life, you try to anticipate the outcome of each decision and action so that you will know what is coming. Only when you have turned over your direction to the wise part of yourself that speaks through your heart can you release this control. Only when you have seen through divine eyes and have become convinced that you are part of a bigger outcome can you relax and allow life to unfold. Now is the time to change the way you participate in your life. You are supported from within and without when you relax and flow with the stream of life.

Healing Exercise

Relax into a state of deep awareness. Become a leaf floating on the river of life. Smell the fresh, sweet air. Hear the birds singing in the trees. Feel the gentle nudge of the breeze. Float with the flow of the river. Feel yourself shoot around rocks to join a calmer flow beyond. Rest for a while in a shady, calm pool. Swirl in a whirlpool until you are released into the flow again. Patiently stop in a stagnant pool until the cleansing rains come and you are sent along your way again. Notice that there are times when you flow along with others and times when you are alone. At some point along the way, you find that your stream converges with other streams. Together, they create a broader flow. Be present and conscious as you experience each aspect of this moving stream and the many changes of scenery. When you return to this moment, write about what you have experienced. How can you bring that flow into your daily life?

Life Purpose

Living Your Life Purpose

You are here to accept and allow your life to flow in whatever direction you are taken through that higher purpose you sense within you. Living this way inspires others to find their way as well.

Peacemaking

You have come to assist in the process of peace. This may mean bringing peace to individuals, families, organizations, nations, or it may affect the entire earth. Allow yourself to be shown your part in the process.

Assisting Others.

Through your own life experiences, you have learned to release control and live in the flow of life. Now you are available to support others in this same process. This may be about accepting and holding a loving place for others to experience the flow or it may involve creating group opportunities to understand and experience the flow of life.

Facilitating Retreat Experiences

In order to gain perspective in life, it is sometimes necessary to step aside from the day-to-day flow. You may be encouraged to be the caretaker of a place where others can gain this perspective, or you may be called upon to lead and facilitate workshops that encourage others to understand their life path.

Violet

Violet is a combination of blue, red, and white. It is located at the top of the head, also referred to as the crown. The crown chakra opens up and out to the universe. Violet combines the connection to the earth through red, the expression of divine direction through blue, and the divine connection and wisdom through white. The wholeness of life is seen and experienced from this integrated vantage point.

Strengths

Expansiveness

You are not confined to that which is seen as human. You are of the universe. You know yourself, all of yourself. Divine intelligence lives within you and operates through you. You recognize the largeness of others as well as yourself. From this broad perspective, the human attachments are understood and acknowledged. From this plane of existence, there is no jealousy, no hate, no fear, and no reason to doubt. Within the sphere of the divine, you are able to declare, "I am."

Royalty

You are royalty. You were birthed by the Divine. You are claimed by the Divine. A white halo crown signifies your acceptance of your divine inheritance. An energy-coat of many colors graces your form. By these colors, all know the strengths you have acquired through your courage. You accept the divine directive you have received to take your leadership role in this life. You stand in quiet acceptance of your powerful self.

Transmutation

The violet color saturates your aura. Energies that have finished their work on Earth, such as control, fear, and hate are transformed into pure potentiality through the violet. By being present as a carrier of violet, you contribute to the transformational process.

Transceiving

You assist in the process of physical manifestation. In order for thoughts to take physical form in the human experience, they must first reach out into the universal field of potentiality. As these creative thoughts return to you, they enter through the violet crown chakra. They are then translated into usable data by the indigo of the third eye chakra, and then passed on to the blue throat chakra where the divine blueprint takes physical form. Consciously or unconsciously you serve as a transceiver of creative thoughts that are to be born here.

Compassionate Detachment

The strength in the violet color allows you to see life from a divine perspective. Compassion wells up within you as you feel the pain that others suffer as they learn here on the earth. This pain comes because they have not paid attention to the subtle nudges that have come to encourage them to learn what they came here to learn. Pain and loss can make them stop to see the deeper meanings of their existence. You know and accept that pain and suffering is part of the process of learning. You do not try to take the pain away. Instead, you extend understanding and compassion to those who are experiencing separation from their own truth.

Accepting of Support

The support you receive from the divine realm is ever-present to you. You know that you are never without assistance. A host of angels and divine beings stand by to follow your directives. You may have been born feeling this support around you, or you may have recognized it over time. This sense of support has now become so natural to you that questioning its existence doesn't even occur to you. If the human part of you forgets that it has this help, which is just a thought away, you quickly remind it of what you know.

Gratitude and Humility.

Your understanding of who you are and where you have come from allows peace, security, fulfillment, loving relationships, meaning, and support to be ever-present in your life. Gratitude fills you from the inside out. Your humility comes from recognizing your divine source. Compassion and support then extend to your human self, which can sometimes forget its connection to the Divine. Hope springs forth as you see the greater truth of the human existence and recognize the desire and commitment of you and many others to bring the human realm into its finest hour.

Forgiveness

You understand the difficulties of the human life. You forgive those who may treat you unfairly, or who lash out at you from their own pain. This does not mean that you do away with your own boundaries. It simply means that you accept the human condition with all of its lessons.

Lessons

The lessons gained from the color violet center around repairing your disconnection from your earthly existence and your disconnection from your spiritual heritage. The disconnection causes an imbalance that leads to spiritual snobbery, spiritual power used for personal gain, distrust, arrogance, and difficulty manifesting what you desire in your life. Yellow is the balancing color for violet. Breathe in yellow through the top of your head, breathe out violet. Yellow brings human empowerment and clarity to balance divine empowerment and knowing.

Aloofness

Do others feel that you are above them? Do you seem to be floating above the earth, not really hearing what others are saying and not really caring what others are experiencing? The lesson in violet is to connect to the earth as well as the heavens. When you are off in space or connected only to your inner realm, you cannot do your work on Earth. You came here for a reason. Do not miss this opportunity.

Spiritual Snobbery

Because you work in the realms of violet, you have an advanced spiritual understanding. When you are disconnected from your heart center, you may see yourself as more advanced or more spiritually powerful than others. You may wonder why others are so slow in understanding spiritual matters. Those others that you judge may be in the middle of their greatest lessons on earth. What they learn through these experiences is valued highly by those in the spiritual realms. Just because you have claimed the abilities that are part of your spiritual self does not mean that you have completed the process. Come down to Earth. Do your work here. Learn what you came to learn. Without that, your experience here is incomplete.

"Mine Is the Only Truth"

A danger in spiritual work is to decide that you have all the answers. This is a way of saying that Divine Intelligence has no more creating or expanding to do. What you understand now may be only the tip of what is to come. What others intuit or experience, however insignificant it may seem, may be a vital piece to a complete understanding of life. By setting your truth above others, you display your spiritual incompleteness. Turn again to experience the unconditional nature of the universe. What each contributes is valuable. Wherever others are in their process is exactly where they are meant to be. Your responsibility is to do the best you can to complete the work you have come to do without comparing it to anyone else's work here.

Misusing Spiritual Power

You have experienced the power of Spirit. Your intuition and spiritual abilities have been developed. Are you using that information and those abilities to uplift others, or are you using these gifts for your own aggrandizement and power? Is your leadership based on divine principles or personal gain? Since you know what others are thinking and you sense motivations and weaknesses in others, it is possible to manipulate them. This is a misuse of your gifts. This manipulation may be so subtle that you don't know you are doing it. What you do may be hidden behind good deeds or helping others. Be honest with yourself. Know your motivations. Clear out the rationalizations. Great responsibility goes with your spiritual powers. They are to be used to manifest the greater good. Your lesson here may be to open your heart to the truth of what you do. Respect the spiritual gifts that are yours. Unconditional love does not manipulate, coerce, take advantage of vulnerability, or assume that one way is better than another.

Not Wanting to Be Here

Living in the bliss of the spiritual energy can be seductive, even addictive. You know how to move into your imagination, leaving your body behind in order to avoid feeling pain. But, if you leave, who is there to care for the body? How can you learn your lessons if you are not present? If you do not do your work now, you may need to come back again. Finish your work now! Work to shift your belief that the body limits the spirit. Nothing limits the spirit! The body cannot fully contain the spirit. The spirit can inhabit the body, yet it moves out beyond the body. You are multidimensional. From the soul center in your heart, you may find that you live in many dimensions of life at one time. Your spiritual nature is much more adept and creative than you give it credit for. Decide to find out how to live fully present in the body as well as the spirit. By doing this, you will contribute to all of us, for this is the work of our present age.

Lack of Forgiveness

When violet is unbalanced, you may place high expectations on others. Judgment may creep into your thoughts. When others treat you unfairly or take advantage of you, you may find it hard to forgive them. Remember, how you treat others is how you are treating yourself inside. What kind of expectations are you laying on yourself? Are you hard on yourself? How do you judge yourself? Look into the mirror that you have set up for yourself. See yourself clearly. The part of you that places high expectations on you, or judges you is following a pattern set up by authority figures in you childhood. This part of you wants to be sure you follow all the rules, don't get into trouble, and excel in all areas of your life. Help this part of you to understand that there is another way to do this. Ask this part of you to become affirming and supportive, so that the child within you can feel safe and cared for. Take that fearful child into a healing pool that you create in your imagination. Though it looks like water, this pool is filled with unconditional love. Soak in the pool. Allow love to penetrate every cell in your body. Drink from the pool until you are totally satisfied. Invite the one who has expected so much of you, to join you there as well. Stay for as long as you wish.

Healing Exercise

Set aside a day to fast and ask for divine direction. Live in the silence for as long as is possible. Eventually, your clamoring thoughts will subside. Peace will envelop you. You will be resting in the sea of no thought and all thought. Open yourself to divine intervention and divine inspiration. Declare your intention to claim your spiritual gifts and use them responsibly. Allow the wholeness of who you are to fill you up. Clarity and respect for all life will naturally follow your divine connection.

Life Purpose

Spiritual leadership

You will be drawn to teach what you know and how you live to others through spiritual leadership. Ask your heart how this is to come about.

Compassionate Detachment

You are to show others how to live from compassionate detachment. You may have been taught that love means involvement. Too often, this leads to unhealthy attachments that create dependencies which drain and stifle you and others. Detached involvement sounds like a misnomer. Instead, it is a paradox. Both can be true at the same time. You are to bring compassion and detached involvement into every part of your life.

Guidance

What you receive through your spiritual connection can help others on their spiritual path. This is a divine calling. Do not take it lightly or use your gifts irresponsibly. Listen to your inner guidance and proceed with humility and caution.

Transceiving

Turn to the strengths found in violet to understand this aspect of your life purpose.

Transmutation

Again, turn to read about this strength that is found in violet.

White

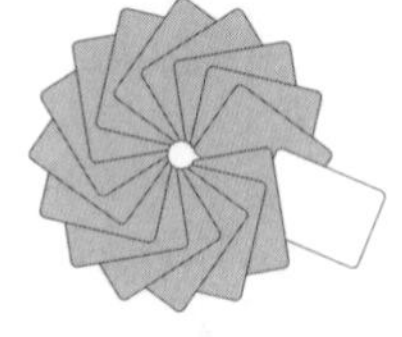

White contains all the colors of light. As with black, all possibilities are available. Black works with these possibilities in the human experience, and white brings in these possibilities through divine energy.

The essence of the Divine Parent is unconditional love. This love is wholeness in action: accepting, creating, waiting, completing, respecting, trusting, fulfilling, and much more. White is the form that this Divine Presence takes when it comes to us in our humanness. Working with white is a way for you to experience Divine Unconditional Love.

White does not serve an energy center of the body. It does not balance another color. However, black and white represent the duality of earth and heaven. White is mixed with other colors to create a combined quality that is different from each of the original colors. For example, red and white make pink. Pink does not have the same force as red, nor does it have the complete essence of unconditional love. Yet, the combination of these colors create a sweetness and loving presence that is welcomed by those who have been wounded, and helps the wounded ones in a way that neither red nor white could.

Strengths

The strength in white comes from its power. This is a power that comes from divine love. It is as if the Source of All Power has sent itself into this dimension to give us access to divine love. With the strength in white, you know, without a doubt, that you are supported, cared for, loved, and assisted from the depths of the universe. With this power, you reflect the nature of love in all its aspects.

Unconditional love

The essence of white is unconditional love that is personal and all-encompassing. You bring that unconditional love to everyone around you. You accept others without judgment. You offer your love without strings attached. You allow others to choose what they are ready to accept. You trust the other person's sense of timing and best pace for his or her transformation. You hold a place of love in your heart for that person, no matter what happens.

Strength

The strength and power of your presence bolster those who have lost hope, and support those who have chosen to move forward at this time. This is not a strength that makes others dependent on you. This is a strength that says, "I'm here for now, until you feel ready to take over." Others feel your strength and know that you will not be taken off course. You will persevere. When others feel this strength in you, they feel more confident to find strength within themselves.

Encouragement

You encourage others to accept themselves as they are. You help them forgive themselves so that they can claim their inner strength and courage and move on.

Trustworthiness

You know others fully. You see the magnificence of their being and the humanness of their struggle. They know that there is nothing they need to hide. You would never take advantage of their vulnerability. With you, they are safe to be just who they are at this moment.

Purity

There are no impurities in you. This does not mean

that you have finished all your lessons. But, this does mean that you recognize imbalance in yourself as soon as it appears. You focus your attention on that lesson immediately. Nothing is left in you that is not being transformed. Therefore, you can be honest and open at all times.

Purposefulness

Your energy is directed and forthright. Your purpose is clear. You are not pushy or demanding, yet you do not stand still. Through white, each color is revealed, as it is needed. You are able to draw on the strengths in all the colors.

Transformation

Just as white is mixed with other colors to create a new vibration, you blend with others to bring about change in the world. Your energies mix with the energies of others to create a force that has its own purpose and abilities.

Divine Direction

Your divine connection is never questioned. It is so clearly part of who you are that it cannot be separated from the rest of you. Sacred living comes from your essence. You appreciate and honor all that has been created. You treat everything in your life with respect, knowing that there is nothing that does not have consciousness. You realize that the same energy that is your Divine Parent is all around you. The form that Divine Energy may take differs, but its essence is the same.

Protectiveness

When appropriate, you create a protective atmosphere for those who are vulnerable. You do this not to make them dependent, but to allow them the space and time to grow into their empowerment. You teach them how to find trust and confidence from within which in time will allow them to create their own protection. You show them how to tap into their own intuitive nature so that they know what is right for them.

Healing

Your loving presence heals whatever it touches. This healing may not be a conscious process; it is who you are. Your touch, your smile, and your compassion move others deeply.

Lessons

When white is unbalanced, the many colors within it can create confusion. When you have lost the connection to unconditional love, you may bottle up tears of despair. Recognizing that your divine connection has been broken begins the shift that brings back the true nature of white.

Confusion

You have lost your way among all the possibilities of your life. Your direction has become unclear. Fear of choosing the wrong path, or believing what is not true, has closed down your inner flow of truth. Discover what has broken your connection to Divine Light. Are you expecting too much of yourself? Are you condemning yourself for your mistakes? Are you afraid you may have to give up something if you follow your life purpose? Ask your heart the truth. Make it your intent to clear up this confusion. Then, ask for help. Your request will be heard.

Despair

When the connection to Divine Light is lost, it is easy to sink into despair. From that dark place, nothing seems possible. There seems to be no way out. Call on Divine Light to surround you and lead you. Ask for clarity and direction. Be ready to take the next step.

Judgmentalism

Are you judging yourself and others? Are you expecting yourself and others to be perfect? Have you forgotten that missing the mark is part of the learning process? Come back to the purity of white. Know that you are where you need to be. What you are experiencing will take you where you need to go. Surrender to that guidance that comes from deep within your soul.

Limited Focus

Focusing on the divine and sacred side of life can become so all-consuming that you lose sight of your human needs and responsibilities. True white never limits your focus. It will take you to the heights of the divine experience without losing sight of the fulfillment found in living your divine purpose on Earth.

Unworthiness

When you feel the unconditional love of the Divine Presence, do you compare that to all the ways you fail to measure up to your own expectations? This is not what is intended. Unconditional love is here to help you feel acceptance. But, you can only take that acceptance in if you open up to it. Forgive yourself, accept yourself, and give yourself some slack. Know that no matter how stuck you feel, you are still accepted and loved. Now love yourself in the same way.

Standing Still

You may have felt that your spiritual life has been at a standstill for some time. The color white suggests that the time of standing still is over. New light is breaking forth. Be prepared to step into this new light. Be prepared to clear away whatever may stand in the way of this next phase in your transformation.

Healing Exercise

Relax and move into a deep part of yourself. Imagine a white column of light coming from above you. Allow it to move down through you and around you. Feel the loving acceptance that cleanses your inner self. Notice how the white transmutes grays and brightens the hue of other colors. Feel the purity and clarity of this presence. Take all of these qualities into yourself. Affirm, "I am pure. I am clear. I am loved. I am loving. I am love." Know that you are all of these and more.

Life Purpose

Leading Others

Spiritual leadership will draw you in no matter where you are. This could be informal leadership among family and friends or as part of an organization.

Healing.

Your presence is healing. Your touch is healing. Your words are healing. You bring these gifts to whatever you do.

Spreading Your Energy

The energy you bring heals all of those around. Consciously work with that energy. Allow it to spread out to those who need it.

Yellow

Yellow is located in the third chakra, the solar plexus. The essence of yellow is empowerment. You know clearly who you are, and you accept your abilities. You feel good about yourself. Violet\purple balances yellow. Yellow brings empowerment to the human self and violet\ purple brings empowerment to the divine self. Yellow brings clarity of thought and violet brings divine clarity.

Strengths

Empowerment of Self

You are clear about who you are. You accept your abilities as part of you. You accept your lessons as the work you came to do in this life. Even when others suggest that you need to change, you are not thrown off course. You trust your inner knowing. You trust the truth that comes through your heart.

Empowerment of Others

You value others. You trust the truth that comes through them. You do not encourage them to change unless they are nudged to do so by their own inner guidance. You are not jealous of their abilities, but instead value what they have to offer. As you see them in their fullness, you offer encouragement for them to be true to themselves.

Clarity

You value your mind. You know that without it you would not be able to use the information that is available. You think very clearly. You communicate your ideas so that they are easily understood. Others ask for your input because they value your thoughtful contributions. You do not use your clear ability to think as a way to devalue someone whose abilities lie elsewhere. You feel compassion for someone who is currently in a mental fog. You help others to value simplicity of thought even when concepts may be complicated.

Practicality

When considering a new idea, you think through how it can be used. If at first a creative thought seems unworkable, you do not dismiss it. You stay with it until you discover how it can be brought into a useable form. Since ideas intrigue you, it would be easy to become engrossed in the thought alone. Instead, you realize that all thoughts come from a creative source beyond you. You look for ways to bring those thoughts down to Earth.

Organization

When working on a project, you plan each step in advance. You are always willing to make changes along the way, but you find that it is easier to work from an overall plan. You have trouble working in confusion and mess. Before anything can be done, you have to organize your space. This helps you to organize your mind.

Originality

Your ideas are fresh and clear. Even old ways of doing things can be seen in a new light. You do not discount what has been done before, but you do look for simple, more practical ways to do the same thing.

Simplicity

You have no need to complicate that which can be made simple. You prefer to go to the heart of the matter quickly. Even with more complicated projects, you break each step down into its simplest parts. You believe that anything can be made understandable when it is presented clearly.

Brightness

You prefer spaces with lots of light. Light, airy spaces help you to breathe and feel free. If you are in cloudy, rainy weather for too long, you begin to crave the sun. Like a sunflower, you reach toward the light, soaking in all the warmth and bright rays as possible. Your disposition is bright and sunny as well. You bring sunshine into any room you enter. Others enjoy the warmth you radiate.

Intelligence

Your mind works quickly and easily. You understand new ideas fully. You take information from a variety of sources, seeing the underlying thread that pulls the ideas together. Often, you catch what others might have missed. When you dig into a field of ideas, you want to go deeply into each part, not just skim the surface. You have no trouble maintaining focus. At times, you do not even hear what is happening around you.

Acceptance of Others

Though you are bright, you do not look down on others who work with ideas more slowly. You listen to their ideas with interest, knowing that there may be a gem waiting to be found. You find the variety in people a delight. How boring it would be if we were all the same!

Openness

You have nothing to hide. You are open with your ideas and your feelings. You comfortably share who you are with others. You are open to knowing another person. You do not have to be the center of attention.

Humor

You laugh easily and openly. You enjoy a good joke or a funny story. You are a good storyteller yourself. You know just when to pause to give the punch line its punch.

Physicality

You like to play sports of all kinds. You like to move your body. You jog, you dance, and you play tennis. You enjoy games that cause you to think, such as chess. You are more comfortable when the game involves a small group than you are with team sports.

Clear boundaries

You know how to say no without acting dictatorial. From the beginning, you are clear about what you will and won't do. You follow through on what you say. Others know exactly where they stand with you. They are comfortable with your boundaries.

Justice

You are fair in all your dealings. You treat everyone with respect. You value everyone's contribution so that others feel included in decision-making. If you feel that others have been unjust, you speak up. If you feel that a government or company system treats people unfairly, you get involved. You would never knowingly be part of a system that would cause you to sacrifice these values.

Lessons

When yellow becomes muddy, insecurity sets in. Lack of clarity, misuse of intelligence and power, hiding information, and acting jealous can result. This can come about through a shaky foundation in the first chakra (red).

Mental Confusion

You have trouble understanding information. The logic of an argument escapes you. You have trouble making decisions, and even when you have made a decision, you question whether it was the right one. You may find that there is a spontaneous part within you that was told that it wasn't smart or didn't know how to make a decision. You have bought into what others thought of you. Now is the time to gather in that little one. Let it know that you are as smart as you need to be and that you have a very capable part of you that can make decisions. Bring this child into your heart. Ask this child to let go of the criticism and shame he or she has experienced. Let her know how much you value her. Ask him to learn to play instead of worry.

Giving Away Power and Control

You let others make decisions for you. You trust what they say and accept what they know more than you trust yourself. You have given away your power. You are allowing others to control you. In doing this, you are not taking responsibility for yourself. Decide now to be who you are. Decide now to make your own decisions, even if some of them turn out to be lessons for you. Take back the responsibility for yourself. What you have to offer is valuable. No one else is just like you. No one else can make the same contribution that you make.

Lack of Boundaries

In order to be liked and accepted, you have given away too much of yourself. You have agreed to help someone when it was not convenient. You have given away something you were not ready to part with. You have not valued your time or your money. This leads to resentment within you, and leads to lack of respect from others. Your strength is in your clarity. Setting boundaries does not mean that you are being unloving. In fact, just the opposite is true. When you are clear about your boundaries, when you are clear about what you will do and not do, when you are clear about what you want, you allow the other person to become clear as well. Not setting boundaries actually takes away another person's ability to decide and act. They feel like they have to read your mind. Figure out what you want. It is time to decide what is okay and not okay for you. Then, speak up clearly. Write out the information if that will help you and others stay clear.

Losing Yourself

If you are not clear within yourself, it is easy to become caught up in someone else's game plan. Soon, you feel that your life is not your own. You are focusing on what that other person wants and needs, not what you want and need. It's okay to focus on your needs. In fact, you will be a better friend and companion if you do fill your own needs first. This does not need to exclude the other person's needs. In any relationship, both persons' needs must be taken into account. But, when you don't fill your own needs, you expect them to be met by someone else or you begin to blame others for what they are doing or not doing. Listen to your heart. Know what you need. Be your own best friend so that you can then be a good friend to others.

Focusing on Details

If you have lost your clarity, you may become focused on the details. You fear that you will forget something or miss a detail. When this happens, it is time to sit quietly while taking in the bigger picture. Then, go back to the steps and the details. Write them down if you need to, but trust that your inner guidance system will remind you of anything you have missed.

Feeling Overwhelmed

When your boundaries are not in place, you tend to take on too much. You don't even know what you've done until overwhelm sets in. Then, you become immobilized. You have to let someone else down, or work so hard that you burn yourself out. It is far better to take the time to consider the whole picture before you begin. Measure your time and energy. Be sure you can still balance your life with other things if you take on this project. Say "No" to it if you don't see a way to keep your balance. Sometimes shifting the due date for a project will allow you the time to deal with it properly.

Spinelessness

When you have lost your center, you have no will. This means that your drive is gone, your direction is confused. Others see you as giving up. In reality, you have allowed emotions or old messages to bind you up. When you know clearly what you are to do, you have no trouble moving forward. Reclaim your center. Reclaim your direction. Make sure that your connection to the earth is in place and your divine direction is leading you.

Inability to Assimilate

When there is confusion, you have a hard time taking things in. This can be ideas, emotions, or nutrition. In a sense, your whole system shuts down. Until you find your inner clarity, the confusion will persist, and you will not be receiving that which keeps you healthy and balanced.

Power Tripping

When you feel you have lost your way, you feel scared and alone. Nothing seems to make sense. The only way you can find to feel more secure is to order your environment. This means that you attempt to control others, yourself, and things around you. You may think that this makes things easier, but in reality, this breeds resentment. The only way to have real power is to be integrated and connected within yourself. Then, power turns to empowerment. Fear turns to trust. There is no need to have power over others or over things, because you can trust that what comes will be exactly what is needed in the right timing.

Impracticality

When you are unable to think clearly or see the consequences of your decisions or actions, you become impractical. What seems like a good idea may actually take you where you don't want to go. Money and time you spend may be wasted. You may find yourself starting one project, but leaving it to start another before the first has been finished. Find out what is standing in the way of your clarity. Are you trying to please someone else? Are you living up to inner expectations that do not fit? Are you bucking your own inner gifts? Clearing up the source of the confusion will bring greater clarity.

Requiring Justice

You are just and expect others to be just like you. This will lead to disappointment. Expectations always lead to disappointment. Come from your own integrity. Allow others to deal with their integrity in their own way. Be clear about what you want. Surround yourself with those who respect others. Know that follow-through will not always be there as you would hope. Remember that everyone is in his or her own process.

Healing Exercise

Imagine a clear, bright day in summer. Allow the sun to penetrate your cells. Let the sun burn out anything that stands in the way of your clarity and truth. Breathe in the sun; breathe out the color of violets. Breathe in the beauty of the sunflower; breathe out the softness of heather. Free yourself to move into the center of the sun. Become its brightness. Become its power. Feel your strength within. Affirm your mental clarity. Affirm your practical abilities. Affirm your clear decision-making. Bring the power of the sun into each of these areas. Do this more than once. Do the exercise as often as you need to, until you can maintain that sunshine within you.

Life Purpose

Power.

Your life purpose will lead you into places of power. You will be asked to make decisions and bring leadership to whatever is being done. Stay close to your inner truth. Do not compromise your integrity.

Seeking Justice

You will be called on to carry a torch for justice. Do this from the heart, not as a battle. Bring justice in through people first. Organizations and government will follow. Help people make choices that affect their own lives; then, they can affect the larger world.

Bringing in Light

You will be asked to bring light to places of darkness and clarity to places of confusion. You will show others how to be powerful from an empowered place within. You will help organizations develop clear boundaries and just expectations.

Hope

You will bring hope and strength where there has been despair and weakness. You will show others how to find their internal power.

Laughter

You will bring joy and laughter with you wherever you go. Your smile will brighten the space you are in. Others will look forward to your presence.

Attention to Detail

Your abilities allow you to pay attention to all the details. You don't miss anything. Your life purpose will use this ability. Where others might develop the overall concept, you know the steps to get there.

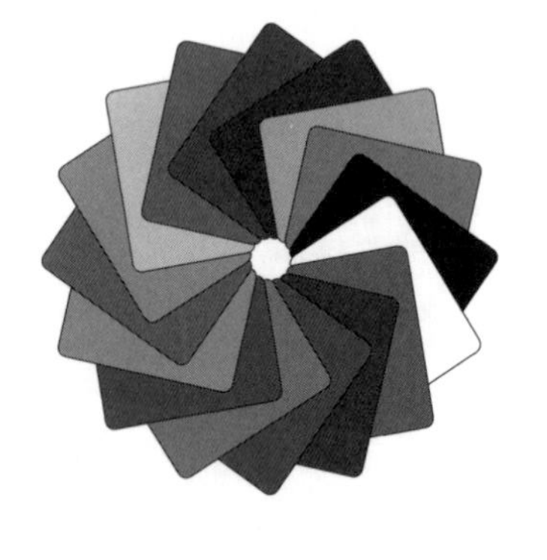

The ColorCards™ Story

It was nearing the end of my first year of training to become a healing facilitator and spiritual guide at Immanuel House in Seattle, Washington, when I became fascinated with color and its healing properties. The "final exam" that first year (spring of 1994) was to use a healing technique that felt important to me. Without understanding why, I chose to work with color to activate the chakra energy centers.

From then on, I began to read more and more about chakras and the use of color in healing. I knew that each color carried its own vibration, just like sound did. I knew that working with the chakra energy centers could reveal physical, emotional, mental, and spiritual blockages; but how could I best use that knowledge?

One day while looking for a deeper understanding of myself by using the Medicine Cards (by Jamie Sams and David Carson), it occurred to me that colors contain meaning within them just as animals do. If a person were to choose colors intuitively, those colors would tell a story about that person's life.

I shared my idea with my transformational group at Immanuel House. They were enthusiastic. Armed with that encouragement, I decided to move forward with my idea by making color cards out of colored construction paper glued onto stiffer paper. Fourteen colors came to me. (These are the same fourteen colors that I used in the first set of Colorcards™.) I explained the layouts that had come to me to my first volunteer. From what I knew about the color and from what I intuited from the color's position in the layout, I began to tell people about themselves. To my delight, my volunteer was amazed. She had learned something important from the experience. Others gathered around to participate. I was encouraged to move my project forward. I felt blessed with a wonderful gift.

Soon, however, procrastination set in. How could I know all that should be said about each color? Who was I, a novice in using color, to think that I could write something meaningful that could open others to their truth?

In spite of my doubt and fear, I determined to go forward. This project felt right. Was I to turn my back on this gift? No. So, I took a week's vacation from my job in order to have plenty of time to stay with the creative energy.

Then, I froze. All the old doubts reappeared. For two days, I combed through every book I had read about chakras and color. I correlated all the information I found. I thought I would then know what to say about each color. However, when I began to write, the words were stilted and cold.

Feeling stuck, I called Jane Lister Reis who was my mentor at Immanuel House. She told me that what I would be given from my inner guidance would be exactly right for my Colorcards™. If someone else were to write about them, what they wrote would be exactly right for them.

I returned to my computer determined to move through the fear and doubt. I placed the color cards in front of me one by one. I read over the compiled information about each color. Then, I simply moved into the color, becoming one with it. I began to write what I felt and experienced with that color. Later, when I read over what I had written, I realized that what I had said about each color was true for the color, but also mirrored what I had learned through my own experience of transformation.

Finally, the writing was finished. Then, the Colorcards™ just sat on my desk. Periodically, I would take them with me to a retreat and do Colorcards™ Readings. They were always well received. Yet, I still procrastinated. Then one day, I realized that I had moved through the fear of not knowing what to write, but had not faced my fear of criticism. What would others say when the Colorcards™ were published? What would my family say? Would others criticize my interpretation of color? I had to talk to that little child inside who had always avoided criticism by being a "good girl." I finally convinced her that even if criticism came, she would not have to deal with it. The grown-up part of me was capable to deal with anything that came.

I set a goal for myself. I determined that I would have the book revised, proofread, and ready to be copied by the end of the summer 1995.

Hurdles such as how to laminate the cards and how to formulate the proper colors presented themselves. Mixing tempera paint didn't work. Finally, I went back to laminating colored paper. Finding the right colored paper was no easy task.

What a glorious day it was when the first version was copied and the cards were laminated and ready to sell! How gratifying it was to find that my friends used the cards often.

Still there was the question of whether the Colorcards™ could be sold in a broader market. I had to take that leap of faith. I had the book and cards printed. I found that there was a broader audience for this work. The Colorcards™ continued to sell steadily.

Now, I offer you the second version of the ColorCards™. The concept is the same, but the information is broader and deeper. Since I have learned more from each vibration, I am now able to share more information with you.

Two new colors have presented themselves to me: lime green and magenta. When lime green first came to me in meditation, I was reluctant to use it. As I journaled about this fear, I found that there was tremendous power in lime green. If this color is not divinely balanced, it can be a power that holds others in bondage or misuses its position. Intuitively, I learned to balance lime green first with violet and then with magenta. Using the two colors together helped me to accept the power of the lime green.

I had also learned to use an additional layout of cards. The layout looks like the cross with the heart at the center, a connection above to the heavens, below to the earth, on the left (as if the person were standing in front of you so it's actually the right side of the body) to the male energy and on the right (also as if the person were standing in front of you so it's actually on the left side of the body) to the female energy. Balance has become the new theme. As we return to wholeness, we must first bring the dualities of this plane into balance.

Though I strayed away from color for awhile developing a system called Inner Reality Therapy™, I now find that color therapy and Inner Reality Therapy™ work perfectly together. Vibrational change is always at the heart of transformation. Color is a perfect mode to use for that transformation.

I offer this story to encourage you to follow where you are led. Whatever you feel passionately, triggers your life purpose. Whatever is brought to you has meaning. Take courage! Push through the fear and doubt. You will never regret it.

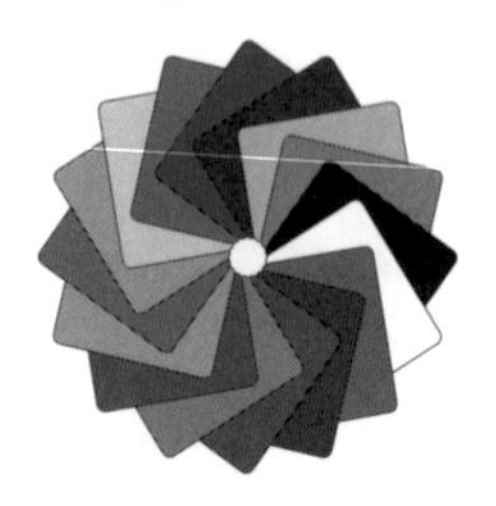

About the Author

Arlene Arnold is a teacher, counselor, and writer. In her work, she uses "tools" she learned through her own inner growth process. Many of the insights gained in this transformational process are included in the ColorCards™.

Arlene was trained as a public school teacher. She loved working with junior high age youth, but always felt drawn to something else. Besides her teaching experience, she has over a decade of experience in business leadership and management. In addition, she completed a training program to become a Spiritual Guide and Healing Facilitator. Through many life experiences, including her own inner spiritual growth, she has come to understand that her work is about personal transformation. Visualizing color later became part of her teaching and counseling. Read "The ColorCards™ Story" (pages 147-150) to see how this fascination with color led to producing the ColorCards™.

For other transformational tools, read and listen to Arlene's "Meditation Tools Made Simple, Techniques to Awaken the Spirit Within" which includes a book and tapes.

Workshops, seminars, newsletter, and products offered by Transformational Tools Made Simple™ may be accessed through Arlene's web site, www.ArleneArnold.com

Notes

Vibrational Tools Available

Meditation Tools Made Simple
Techniques to Awaken the Spirit Within

Book and 4 (four) taped meditations
Learn to relax, center, connect to your inner guidance and release what holds you back!
$23.95

Mini ColorCards™
Cards and booklet to carry in your pocket!
Pick a card for the day – use a simple layout to work with your inner balance
$7.50

Workshops, Classes, Intensive Training

www.ArleneArnold.com
P.O. Box 3633
Federal Way, WA 98063
(206) 781-5791

Finding Your Life Purpose

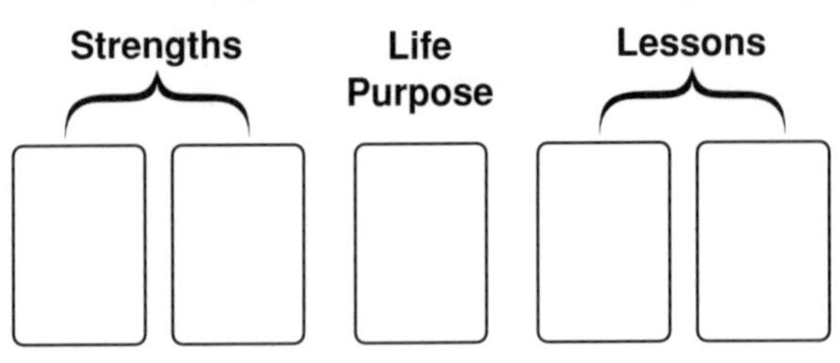

DATE:______________

Write the color of each card selected on the cards above

Strengths

Interpretation: ____

____

____

Interpretation: ____

____

____

Life Purpose Card

Interpretation: ____

____

____

Lessons:

Interpretation: ____

____

____

Interpretation: ____

____

____

What does this layout say to you about where you are in your life, where you are heading, and what you need to do next?

Understanding Situations in Your Life

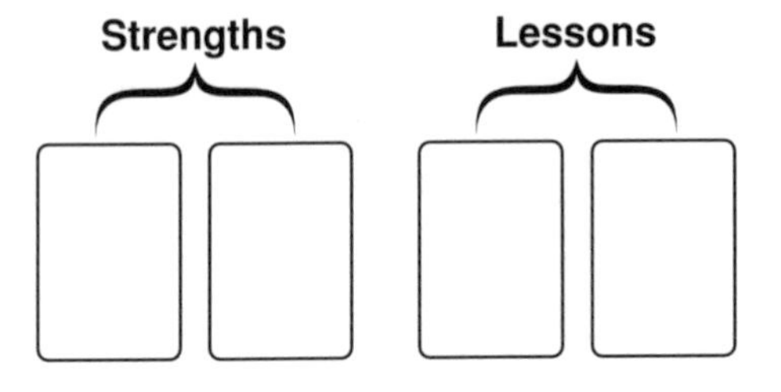

DATE:______________

In one sentence, write about the situation you want to understand.

____

____

____

____

Write the color of each card selected on the cards above; below, and on the next page, summarize their meaning.

Strengths:

Interpretation: ____________________________

____

____

____

Interpretation: ____________________________

____

____

____

Lessons:

Interpretation: ______________________________

Interpretation: ______________________________

What do these colors tell you about your Life Challenge?

Working with Balance in Your Life

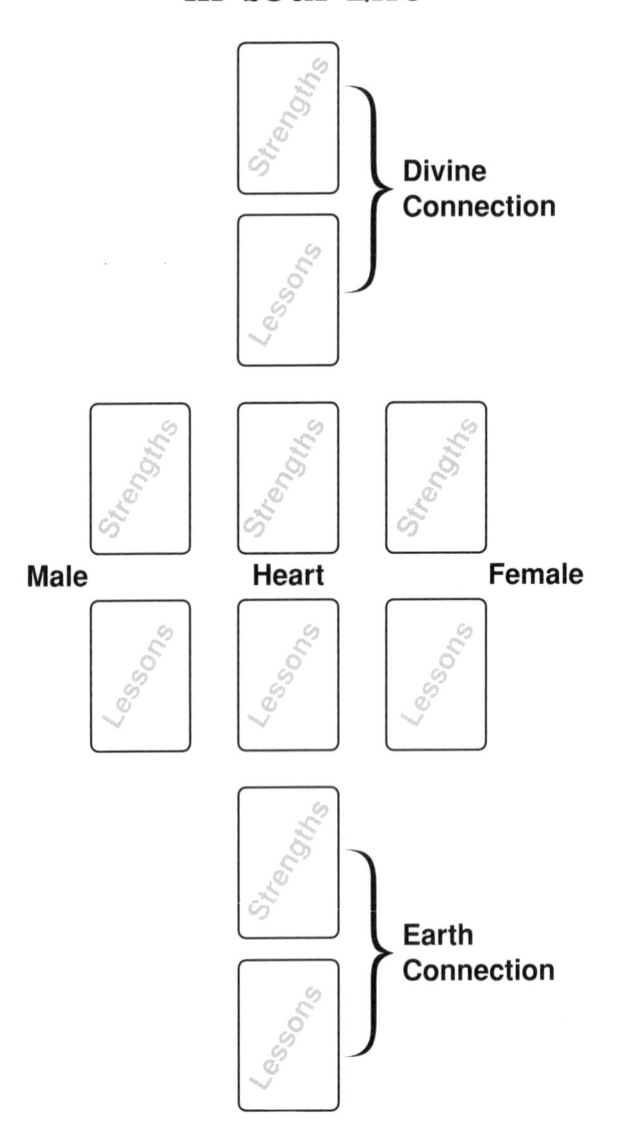

DATE:________________

Write the color of each card selected on the layout sheets. Summarize what you learn from each card.

Divine Connection

Strength: ____

____

Lesson: ____

____

Heart:

Strength: ____

____

Lesson: ____

____

Male:

Strength: ____

____

Lesson: ____

____

Female:

Strength: ____

____

Lesson: ____

____

Earth Connection:

Strength: ____

____

Lesson: ____

____

Notice what is out of balance. Based on the information in the cards. Write about what you have learned from this imbalance. Create an intention to shift that balance.

Notes

Notes

Notes

Notes

Notes